Why Does My Dog Drink Out of the Toilet

Other books by John Ross and Barbara McKinney

Dog Talk: Training Your Dog Through a Canine Point of View

Puppy Preschool: Raising Your Puppy Right—Right from the Start!

John Ross
and
Barbara McKinney

John Ross and his daughter, Hannah,
with their four dogs:
Drifter, Bentley, Crea, and Byron

Why Does My Dog Drink Out of the Toilet

Answers and Advice
for All Kinds
of Dog Dilemmas

St. Martin's Press

New York

WHY DOES MY DOG DRINK OUT OF THE TOILET? Copyright © 1997
by John Ross and Barbara McKinney. All rights reserved. Printed in
the United States of America. No part of this book may be used or
reproduced in any manner whatsoever without written permission
except in the case of brief quotations embodied in critical articles
or reviews. For information, address St. Martin's Press,
175 Fifth Avenue, New York, N.Y. 10010.

Design by Judith Stagnitto Abbate

Library of Congress Cataloging-in-Publication Data

Ross, John.
    Why does my dog drink out of the toilet? : answers and advice
for all kinds of dog dilemmas / John Ross and Barbara McKinney.
        p.   cm.
    Includes index.
    ISBN 0-312-15692-8
    1. Dogs—Behavior.   2. Dogs—Training.   I. McKinney, Barbara.
II. Title.
SF433.R83   1997
636.7—dc21   96-6552
                                                                     CIP

First Edition: June 1997
10   9   8   7   6   5   4   3   2   1

This book is dedicated to our four wonderful dogs,
Byron, Bentley, Drifter, and Crea.
Thank you for making life better.

Acknowledgments

SPECIAL THANKS TO OUR FRIENDS and clients who captured with a camera the dogs they love so well:

Darren Beylouni and Remi
Marietta Christie and Princess
Mike Cody and Polo
Debbie Corcione and Joshua
Lori Crosby and Lexi, Lola, and Dundee
Wayne Crosby and Carrie
Diana Graves and Mookie
Joyce Jaskula and Cork and Glin
Pamela Lape and CB, Molly, and Wally
Alyssa Lima
Bonnie Mathewson and Tuffy, Dolly, Fluffy, and Dixie
Rita Lee Mignosa and Henry, Cosmo, and Francis
Gail Nopper and Penny
Maryjane Osborne and Margaret
Susan Phillips and Linus
Janice Quigley and Tess
Jennie Scaife and Monty
The Stieglitz family and PJ
Lynn Tucker and Cozner
Jennifer Wiegand and Riley and Alexandra
Julie Wiese
Karl Wiese

We also want to thank Steve McCluskey (again), owner of the Company of the Cauldron, for consistently having great food and ambience; Susie, Tracy, and Cosmo Root of Cioppino's for Nantucket bay scallops and other fine fare; Sweet Inspirations for coconut truffles; and—when on the road—the Harbor House on Sanibel Island for stone crabs, and Louie's Backyard in Key West for grilled grouper sandwiches, cold beer, an awesome view of the ocean, and a table overlooking the dog beach.

Thanks also to our great editor, Bob Weil, who probably didn't realize at first how much we had to say about dogs.

Contents

Breeds and Breeding

Good Handling and Training Tips 47

Behavioral Problems 73

Introduction

THIS BOOK IS A RESPONSE to questions that owners ask me about their dogs. The questions first appeared in my newspaper column, "Dog Talk," which appears in *The Nantucket Beacon,* on Nantucket Island, Massachusetts. It's a popular column and has been a great format to hear about all sorts of canine problems.

The questions I'm asked range from feeding schedules to crate training to aggressive biting. Some of the problems are funny—like why does my dog drink out of the toilet? (see page 31). Some of the questions are sad. Most are serious enough that the owner needs help—but not so bad that they can't be solved with some professional advice. If you own a dog, you probably will recognize yourself (or someone you know) in many of the questions. That's because dog owners face a lot of the same problems. And we all want pretty much the same thing from our dogs: a well-behaved friend who brings joy and companionship to our lives.

When I'm teaching a dog obedience class, I've found that when one person asks a question about their dog, everyone in the class learns something. The same has proved true of my question-and-answer newspaper column. That's why this book will help every dog owner be better at understanding, controlling, and appreciating their dog.

Of course, every dog owner will not have every problem described here. But they probably will deal with many of them during their pet's ten-to-fifteen-year lifetime. And it's not just during puppyhood or adolescence that problems pop up. Even a well-trained, older dog can demonstrate some puzzling (or infuriating!) behavior. Drifter, my eleven-year-old Australian shepherd, *still* steals food when he finds an opportunity to get away with it. My biggest frustration is that he seems to have taught everything he knows to Crea, my two-year-old springer spaniel. So his legacy will live on, while I'm securing the trash can and dinner leftovers until I'm sixty.

You get the idea. Owning a dog is an adventure. This book will definitely help you—or someone you know—cope with rough spots in the road. I sincerely hope that it smooths the path enough so that the road you and your dog travel together is a long and memorable one.

JOHN ROSS
Nantucket Island, Massachusetts
August 1996

I travel on the song lines that only dreamers see
Not known for predictability

Jimmy Buffett
"Barometer Soup"

Everyday Living

A Good Family Dog

DEAR DOG TALK: I'd like to get a dog for my family. My wife and I have three children—two girls (seven and five) and a son, three. Do you suggest that we get a puppy, or should we adopt an older dog? Should it be a male or female? Should it be purebred or a mutt? We've been looking at dog books and the kids like the Siberian huskies, but my wife prefers a smaller dog. Any advice would be appreciated.

DEAR FUTURE DOG OWNERS: My standard answer when parents with young children ask me what is the best dog for their family is, "Get a stuffed dog!" That sounds harsh, but here's why I feel this way. Parents with small children are usually too busy to deal with the many demands of feeding, exercising, and training a dog. That's especially true when the dog is a puppy. Puppies have a lot of needs, especially the need to be supervised constantly. That's hard to do in a household with small children.

In addition, most young children (before the ages of eight or nine) cannot share the responsibility of exercising or training a dog. They're too young to convince any dog that they're in charge. Dogs think of small children as submissive littermates that they can climb on, mouth their arms and legs, and steal their food. Adults in the household must prevent this, which means the parents must supervise the kids *and* the dog *and* all interactions between the two. That's a lot of extra work.

My best advise is to wait until your youngest child is eight years old. Older kids don't need the same supervision with a dog that young children do. Also they're old enough to help with feeding, grooming, and even training. Sharing the responsibility among all family members makes a pet-owning experience that much more enjoyable for everyone.

In the meantime, you can develop your children's interest in dogs. Read dog books with them and watch movies and videos about dogs. For a family outing, spend a day at an all-breed dog show and obedience trial. If you have friends with sweet-natured, well-trained dogs, let the kids visit with their dogs. These are just a few of the ways you can enjoy dogs as a family before you take on the responsibility of raising one.

However, I never like to underestimate the abilities of individuals. I'm sure there are people out there with small children and dogs who get along just fine. But because of my profession, I'm the guy who hears all the stories of chaos and disaster, and I've heard a lot of them!

Here are the answers to your other questions, which will be useful when you and your family are ready for a dog. Is a puppy a good choice? When you raise and train a dog from the time it's eight weeks old, you stand a better chance of ending up with a nice adult pet. That's because the first year of a dog's life is a formative time. If you handle and train the puppy right, you control how the dog "turns out" as an adult. But as I mentioned earlier, that first year is a lot of work. You have to live through puppyhood, which means dealing with housebreaking, chewing and mouthing, introducing basic obedience, etc. Dogs don't get their full adult personality until they're around two years old.

When you adopt an older dog, you risk inheriting other people's mistakes. People usually don't give up well-behaved, sweet, wonderful dogs for adoption. If you are fortunate enough to adopt a well-trained older dog, you can save yourself a tremendous amount of work by not having to go through the "growing up" process. Although, in theory, an older dog is a riskier proposition, many rescue organizations throughout the country successfully place older dogs with families every year. I'm glad they do. Giving an unwanted dog a home is a wonderful, loving act. If you take this route, be very clear to the adoption agency about what you expect from a dog. In your household, for example, you would need to be sure to find a dog tolerant of kids. Then be prepared to help the dog adjust to its new life.

As far as male versus female, I've successfully raised and trained both. I've found neither gender to be more intelligent than the other, although males have a tendency to "test" their owners more than females do. Most male dogs instinctively assume that one day it will be their turn to "lead the pack." Females find a place in the family and are usually content to stay there. Neutering the male dog helps tremendously to curb this testing tendency, not to mention its many other benefits.

Tess, a golden retriever, radiates sweetness. If you want a larger breed for a family dog, goldens make wonderful pets.

As far as mutt versus purebred, that's up to you. With a purebred, it's easier to predict what a puppy's size and temperament will be as an adult. For example, if you specifically want a protective dog, your chances of getting one are greater if you buy a purebred German shepherd than any old black-and-tan mutt. If you want a "marshmallow" who's gentle with the kids, a golden retriever is a good bet. If you want a "moose," you can be sure that a Great Dane will be big! Mutts are certainly less predictable. However, I've met *lots* of mixed-breed dogs over the years. They're every bit as smart and beautiful as purebreds, and they're a lot less expensive!

Finally, you asked about Siberian huskies. They are truly one of the most beautiful purebred dogs. On the other hand, I've found them to be one of the most difficult breeds to train. If I were in your situation and felt strongly about getting a dog now, I'd get a Labrador or golden retriever (or, for smaller breeds, a West Highland terrier or poodle) and, of course, a copy of my training books, *Puppy Preschool* and *Dog Talk*. I'd also enroll in a crash-course seminar on patience and perseverance!

Training an Older Dog

DEAR DOG TALK: Can you still train an older dog? I have a mixed shepherd-Lab who is five years old. She's not too bad, and she is very sweet-natured. I'd like her to come better when I call and also to stop pulling on the leash when she sees another dog.

DEAR OPTIMISTIC: You have every reason to be optimistic! I don't believe in the cliché "You can't teach an old dog new tricks." As a matter of fact, one of the best dogs to come through my training classes was a thirteen-year-old beagle. It is true that it's easier to train a dog if you start during puppyhood, and new tricks or behaviors are always easier to establish than old habits are to break. But with patience and perseverance, I'll bet you can succeed.

The one factor that makes training an adult dog extremely difficult, if not impossible, is violent resistance. If a dog is going to attack the trainer every time the trainer tries to make him do something, the prognosis for success is poor. However, your sweet-natured dog probably doesn't fit into this category.

For the things you would like to accomplish with your dog—coming when called and not pulling on the leash—there are specific training techniques that will help you do this. Enroll in a course that will teach you these procedures, or read how to do it in *Dog Talk*. Then get out there and practice with your dog! Don't assume that it's too late to start. You and your dog still have many years together. Those years will be even more enjoyable if you teach her better ways to behave.

Teaching a Dog to Swim

DEAR **DOG** **TALK:** We just got a standard poodle puppy. One of the books we read about the breed said that they were originally bred as water dogs. What is the best way to teach her how to swim?

DEAR **POODLE** **PARENTS:** You do not need to teach your puppy how to swim. Dogs instinctively know how. (Most dogs, that is! Bulldogs will sink like a rock. Their short legs and hefty body conformation are not conducive to swimming.) But a standard poodle and other breeds with a more typical canine body shape can certainly swim.

You job will not be to teach your puppy how to swim, but to build her confidence so that she enjoys swimming. Sometimes this takes time, so don't be in a hurry. Don't force her into the water in any way. Do *not* do the classically stupid act of throwing her in! Gentle introduction is important, but not everyone seems to realize this.

One summer I was walking along the beach and saw a young couple walking with a golden retriever puppy who was only about eight weeks old. It was high tide and large waves were crashing on the beach. Every time a wave hit the beach the puppy flinched and acted really frightened. If they thought they were getting their pup used to the water, they were dead wrong. The puppy was only learning to be more fearful.

Or consider this story. A couple of years ago I taught obedience training at a camp for dogs and their owners in Vermont. The camp had a fellow who offered "doggie swimming lessons." His technique was to pick the dog up, carry it into the water about level with his chest, and then gently lower the dog into the water. The dog would then frantically swim to shore. A woman with a seven-month-old black Lab pup had participated in the swimming class that morning. I remember asking her, "Did your puppy learn how to swim this morning?" Her reply was, "I think he *knew* how to swim. Today I think he learned never to let anyone pick him up near water again!" As gentle as this method seemed, it did not work. I've seen time and time again that forcing dogs into the water only frightens them.

Here's the way to do it right. Take your puppy to a gentle stream, pond, bay, or other calm water. Sit by the water's edge and just let your

With proper introduction to the water, most dogs love to swim. Alexandra, an English shepherd, is an exuberant water dog, even though her breed specializes in land-based activities,
such as herding sheep.

puppy play near you. After a few sessions of doing this, bring your pup's
favorite ball or squeaky toy. Play a game of fetch by the edge of the water.
Innocently let the toy land an inch or two in the water. Praise your puppy
enthusiastically if she goes in after it. If she does not want to get it, you
should get it. Let her see that the water is no big deal. Do this every day
for a couple of weeks. As she becomes braver, let the toy land a few inches
farther out.

If it's a hot day and the pond or stream is good for swimming, you can
sit in the water just covering your legs. This may encourage her to come
in. If it does, praise her, but do not coax her if she is hesitant. Strange as it
seems, coaxing only makes dogs resist more. Say nothing until she comes
in on her own, *then* praise her.

As your pup becomes braver, you can edge out a little deeper. If she
does follow you into deeper water, *be very careful* if you get to where the
water is over your head. Dogs will sometimes try to climb up on you. Your
dog's toenails can scratch you, and a large dog could push you under water.
The situation could quickly become dangerous.

If you have a friend with a dog who loves to swim, let your puppy watch this dog swim. Watching another dog swim often builds a puppy's confidence. When your puppy finally does swim, do not be dismayed if she flaps her front feet out of the water and splashes. It often takes experience before dogs learn to keep their front feet underwater and swim gracefully.

If you take your time and introduce your dog to water in a positive, gradual way, I'm sure she will learn to love swimming. I've owned several different breeds of dogs over the years and each of them loved swimming because I took this approach. It does takes time, and you must be patient, but their enjoyment of the water is worth it. My late German shorthaired pointer, Jena, did not become a proficient swimmer until she was over a year old. But once she got it, she was like a seal! She truly could swim circles around any Lab or golden I knew. Our black Lab, Byron, was almost eight months old before he got the hang of it. Barbara was so proud of him she made him a certificate of achievement for his crate. I even owned a bull mastiff who loved to swim.

There may be someone reading this column saying, "Yeah, right. I threw old Hammerhead out of the boat when he was a puppy and he loves to swim." My response is that he learned to swim *despite* your bad handling! Of course there's always an exception to every rule, but it's not worth the risk and I've met too many dogs who were traumatized by such an approach. Take your time and do it right. Your puppy's future as a water-loving dog depends on it!

Dogs in Pickup Trucks

DEAR DOG TALK: My brother reads your column every week because he loves dogs. He also likes you and agrees with your training advice. Maybe you can clue him in because he won't listen to me. Isn't it risky for him to let his Rottweiler puppy ride in the back of his pickup truck?

DEAR SMART SISTER: It's not only risky, it's downright dangerous. I realize it is the "vogue" in many communities to have a dog cruising around in the back of the pickup. But if horror stories impress you, give a call to any animal hospital in those communities. Ask them about some of the dogs they have put back together. All "pickup dogs" need to do is spot a rabbit or another dog—and out they go. If the dogs live, broken legs, fractured skulls, and damaged spines are often the result. The most common expression the veterinarian hears is, "He never did *that* before." It's not worth the risk of injury and suffering to your innocent animal. Buy a harness and restraint for your dog or put him in the cab with you.

Crumbs All Over the House

DEAR DOG TALK: How can I train my dog not to break up his Milkbone into several pieces and scatter them all over the house? I've tried scolding and starving him to correct him and nothing seems to work!

DEAR FRUSTRATED: There are some things that even John Ross can't train a dog to do! This might be one of them. Most dogs have harmless little idiosyncrasies that are difficult to change. Your dog's snacking habit does not sound serious, but if it bothers you, here are a few things you can try.

To overcome this particular behavior, try breaking up your dog's Milkbones into small pieces and giving him one piece at a time. Or you can buy very small biscuits to start with. If your dog has a kennel crate, you can try giving him the biscuit only in the crate. This may help him form a habit of eating the biscuit in one spot. You could also use a laundry room or similar small room to give him his treats, which will at least confine the mess to one place. I wouldn't scold or starve him. That's not going to teach him anything.

Large Dog in a Condo

DEAR DOG TALK: Do you feel that a Great Dane is too big to live in a condo? Our apartment is rather spacious and there is outdoor space to exercise a dog.

DEAR DANISH: I love Great Danes. Despite their size, most Danes are pretty calm dogs. Although they are large, they spend a lot of time curled up sleeping. Certainly exercise is important with any breed. As I've always said, "Tired puppies are good puppies!" Also check out the dog's mother and father. If they are calm, chances are their offspring will be, too. In my experience, I've found the fawn-colored Danes to be the calmest and gentlest. No matter which color you choose, be sure to take your time and research the breed before selecting a pup.

Tips for Long Car Trips

DEAR DOG TALK: I live in New England, and I'm thinking of driving to Florida with my dog this winter. I've never taken a long trip with my dog before. (She's only two.) Do you think it's a good idea? Do you have any advice?

DEAR SOUTHBOUND: I think it's a great idea. In fact, if there's room in your car, I'll go with you! (Only kidding.) Drifter and I have driven to Florida many times, so I can give you some specific tips as well as some general ones.

First of all, keep your dog's comfort and safety in mind. Pack the car so there's a place for your dog to sleep and to sit comfortably. Some people choose to put their dogs in a crate during a car trip, which is fine. Drifter

**My traveling pal, Drifter, and me in Florida. Road trips with a dog can be great adventures–
and loneliness is never a problem.**

likes to watch the scenery, so he usually rides "shotgun" in the front passenger seat. Take a cooler full of water, your dog's bowl, and an adequate
supply of food. Pack the food so your dog can't raid it when you leave the
car to fill up on gas. (Drifter taught me that one!) Make frequent rest stops
for your dog to eliminate, and be sure to offer him water each time. *Always*
clip your dog to his leash before you open the car door. A loose dog near an
interstate highway can mean disaster. Don't take any chances.

Before you go, check out hotel chains that accept pets. You don't want
to be tired and hungry while searching for a place where you and your dog
can spend the night. I have a few favorite stops en route that Drifter really
enjoys. One is Jekyll Island in Georgia. Its wide beaches make for some
memorable evening hikes and morning runs to stretch our legs. Be fore-
warned: From what I understand, no hotels in South Carolina accept pets.
Check this out before you plan to spend the night there.

When you get to Florida, you'll find that its beaches are not always opened to dogs the way they are here on Nantucket. If you can, make a few phone calls to the towns where you plan to visit to find out their rules on this. Also, Florida's warm climate means that fleas and other parasites are always ready and willing to hop on your New England hound. Check with your vet for collars, sprays, or other items that you should take along to be prepared for this problem. Enjoy your vacation, but don't take a vacation from taking good care of your dog.

Loose Dogs on the Beach

DEAR DOG TALK: I was on vacation at the beach when a big wet and sandy dog ran up to us, jumping on my kids, sniffing around our cooler, walking on our blanket, and dripping on everything. He didn't hurt anything, and he soon left to bother another family. Was I right to get angry over this, or is the beach considered open space for all dogs?

DEAR BEACH BUM: Of course you should feel angry! That dog was a big annoyance, and his owner is completely irresponsible for letting him run loose. It's especially irresponsible in the summer when the beach is crowded with people. I love the beach, and there's nothing like a nice beach walk with a canine pal. But I agree that loose dogs are a problem.

As a trainer, I'm especially annoyed when I see dogs who are not trained to come when called picking fights with dogs being walked on a leash. The loose dogs jump all over other dogs and people as their owners scream, "Come! Come! Come!" to no avail. If your dog does not come when called reliably, use some common sense. Keep him on the leash!

I'm extremely fortunate that the beaches where I live are open to dogs. Many beach communities don't allow dogs on the beach. It's important that owners not abuse this wonderful privilege.

And on another beach-related topic: *Please* be careful when you take your dog swimming. Many ocean beaches have an extremely strong rip and large waves. Some areas are downright hazardous—to humans and dogs alike. Don't assume that your dog can handle it. Keep him out of the surf! I've heard some terrible stories about dogs being swept away. Even strong-swimming Labs and goldens are not safe. If your dog loves to swim, take him to safe waters. Bays, ponds, streams, etc., all offer a refreshing dip. (But depending on what part of the country you live in, be sure to watch out for snapping turtles or alligators!)

Dogs and Toddlers

DEAR DOG TALK: I have a five-year-old golden retriever/Lab mix named Jesse. He is a neutered male that my husband and I have had since he was eight weeks old. He was our "child" until fourteen months ago when our son Joseph was born.

Although we love Jesse dearly, it's hard to give him the same amount of attention he used to receive before the baby was born. When we first brought Joseph home from the hospital, Jesse regressed with some of his training. He chewed up a couple of things and had a housebreaking accident in the living room. He seemed to get over it and appeared to have adjusted to the baby, but in the last couple of weeks he has been grumbling when my son walks over to him.

The first time he did this I scolded him in a loud, firm voice. After that, whenever Joseph came near him, he would act real nervous and start to shake. I praised him to reassure him and he seemed to get his confidence back, but now he is grumbling again. I call this "grumbling" because I'm not sure that he is growling. He never curls his lip or shows his teeth. He has never snapped in his life, even at another dog. Sometimes when I hug him he makes this groaning sound, but his tail wags. I realize this is a long letter, but I'm wondering if you have ever heard of anything like this before. If so, do you have any suggestions on what I should do?

DEAR CONCERNED MOM: It can be difficult to determine exactly what a dog is doing based on an owner's description in a letter or over the telephone. I'll do my best to answer your question, although I recommend that you contact a qualified professional trainer in your area and have that person observe your dog in action.

Assuming that Jesse is actually growling at your son, I would recommend that you continue to verbally correct him. But it is important not to *over*correct him. Your description of your dog getting upset by your loud,

Nicole and PJ, a yellow Labrador retriever, truly adore each other. Toddlers and dogs can usually be friends, as long as there is attentive adult supervision and strict ground rules that require gentle, respectful behavior from everyone.

firm correction—plus your statement that he has never snapped at any-one—indicates that Jesse is a sensitive, submissive dog. Don't be so loud with your correction the next time. Saying "NO" or *"Nhaa!"* in a low, growl-like tone will probably get your message across. Timing is also important. If Jesse shows any signs that he is *about* to growl at the baby, tell him "NO" immediately. This correction will come just as he is thinking about growling and will prevent the growl from ever starting.

It's also important that you help Jesse make a pleasant association with your son. If Jesse likes doggie treats, have Joseph feed him treats a few times a day. Let Joseph help you fill Jesse's bowl at mealtimes. When you take your son for a walk in the stroller, bring Jesse along. This will help Jesse think of the baby as a member of the family, or in canine terms, as a pack member.

It is imperative that you—and all parents—supervise interaction between small children and dogs at all times. In your case, Jesse is approaching middle age and may have sore hips or shoulders. If Joseph lies on Jesse and hurts him, Jesse is not going to be thrilled to see the baby coming his way. Imagine having a sunburn. As soon as someone gets near you, you might growl, "Don't touch me!" It's an understandable response. I'd still correct Jesse for growling at the baby, but I would also start to teach Joseph that there are times when he must leave Jesse alone. Letting a toddler run wild on a dog won't help either of them respect or like each other very much.

Also, try to find ten minutes every day to practice obedience training exercises with Jesse. This will help Jesse feel that he is still special in your life; plus, it will give you more control over him when he interacts with Joseph. I've had people tell me that my obedience training guidelines, which are based on firmness, consistency, love, and praise, are the same ingredients for raising nice children. It sounds like you've made a good effort with Jesse, so keep up the good work with Joseph!

Christmas Presents for the Dog

DEAR DOG TALK: I don't own a dog, but my sister does. She treats her dog like one of the family. I was thinking of getting her dog a Christmas present, but I'd like some tips on what a dog would like. Her dog is a Great Pyrenees—a big fluffy thing named Ajax.

DEAR HOLIDAY ELF: Like humans, dogs love Christmas gifts! But like small children, dogs should only receive gifts that are safe. Squeaky toys are a lot of fun to buy, because they come in so many playful shapes. Large pet supply stores may have a whole wall or aisle of them! Latex squeaky toys are usually better than vinyl, especially for larger breeds, because vinyl toys are easily ripped apart. (Dogs can ingest the pieces, which may become stuck in their throat or belly.) Most dogs also love rawhide bones, although it is important to always supervise while your dog chews them. Do not let them bite off small chunks of rawhide, which also can get stuck in their throats. If you choose rawhide bones, bigger is better. So is real rawhide—as opposed to chopped and pressed rawhide bits. Big dogs crunch those apart in a few bites.

A great gift for any dog is a new training leash and collar and a copy of *Dog Talk: Training Your Dog Through a Canine Point of View.* For a family thinking of getting a puppy, *Puppy Preschool* will start them off on the "right paw."

Holidays can be great fun for dogs, but safety still has to come first. Byron, one of my dogs, chews on a Christmas rawhide.

Here are some important holiday tips: Always supervise dogs (especially puppies) around the Christmas tree. Don't let them eat tinsel or chew the wires on the lights. Chocolate is toxic to dogs. Do not feed it to them, and if you live with a food thief like my Australian shepherd, Drifter, keep all tempting morsels out of reach. This applies to candy dishes on end tables, wrapped food gifts under the tree, and sweet treats in a stocking hung by the chimney with care.

Electric Fences— Pros and Cons

DEAR DOG TALK: What do you think of those electric containment systems designed to keep dogs in the yard?

DEAR FENCE SHOPPER: I think systems such as Invisible Fence are fine as long as the dog is trained properly to the system and the owners use the system responsibly. Actually, owners have several options for keeping their dogs contained. These include traditional fencing, invisible fencing systems, or supervising the dog in the yard coupled with training the dog to come reliably when called. My primary objective is to get owners to *keep their dogs in their yards.* Dogs who run loose get hit by cars, poisoned by substances in garbage pails, fall through ice and drown, etc.

Electric containment systems are designed to condition the dog not to cross the boundary of the yard. The dog wears a collar fitted with a radio transmitter, which gives him a shocklike correction if he leaves the yard. Two or three seconds *before* the dog receives the correction, he hears a beeping sound that warns him that the correction is coming if he does not back up into the yard.

It's absolutely imperative that owners follow the electric fence training procedures, which are designed to ensure success. Specifically, they need to teach the dog to *back up* when he hears the warning tone, not stand in place or continue forward across the boundary. Just putting the radio collar on the dog and releasing him into the yard will not work. Training often requires four to six weeks of daily practice before the dog knows clearly how to respond and can be allowed freedom in the yard.

With these systems, I recommend that owners do not leave their dogs outside all day long when they are not home. These systems are mechanical devices that can fail. If the battery in the collar dies, the collar will not work. If the electricity goes out, so does the system. I've known dogs who test the system every day. They will go to the boundary. If they hear the beep, they quickly back into the yard. If there is no beep, they immediately leave the yard and are off on their own.

Leaving your dog outside when you are not home can be risky in other ways. Someone can pull into your driveway and steal your dog—and yes, I've heard of this happening. Another dog could wander into your yard and start a fight, dig holes, chew up garden items, mate with your dog, harass your cat, and so on.

In addition, being outside all day can even affect a dog's behavior. By doing whatever they feel like doing, with no structure in their lives, dogs tend to become overly independent and unwilling to please. This is counterproductive to having an obedient dog. Although the dog may be staying on your property, he can develop the same attitude as the dog who runs free all day—which is to ignore your commands.

Electronic containment systems do work well if you train your dog correctly. They are handy if you want to be able to open the door and let your dog out to go to the bathroom. They're practical if you want your dog outside with your kids or keeping you company while you work in the yard. However, the system should not be used as a substitute for exercise, bonding, and training.

A Birthday Cake for Dogs

DEAR READERS: This cake was served at a party held at my house to celebrate my black Lab Byron's tenth birthday. Byron and the rest of the canine guests guarantee that it's a sure winner!

Aunt Joycie's Doggie Birthday Cake

MIX TOGETHER:

2 large cans of Pedigree dog food
2 cups of cooked rice
½ cup of dry oatmeal to make firm

An appetizing birthday treat–for dogs. Byron, the Labrador retriever "Birthday Dog," got the first bite, followed by Drifter and the rest of the canine gang.

Place mixture in a springform pan placed directly on a serving tray (without the pan's bottom). Chill in refrigerator 2 to 3 hours. Remove springform pan.

To decorate the top of the cake: Place one fried egg in the center. Use 1 can of sardines and about 4 ounces of cheese (cut into matchsticks) to form "spokes" radiating from the egg. Place 5 hotdogs (sliced as coins) to fill in the spaces between the spokes. Finally, use 1 package of broccoli cole slaw to garnish around platter. Keep chilled until serving.

Serves 8 to 10 (dogs, that is).

Helping a Homeless Dog

DEAR DOG TALK: My neighbor's dog used to run loose all the time. It was taken to the pound so many times that the owner must have given up on the dog. I saw it listed as "adoptable" in our animal shelter's advertisement in the newspaper. For some reason I feel really sad about this situation. Aside from adopting him, is there anything I can do?

DEAR COMPASSIONATE: I wish your experience was rare, but I'm afraid that it's awfully common. I occasionally stop by my local animal shelter. I remember going in one time and had the chance to meet a beautiful, medium-sized terrier mix sitting there behind bars. The folks at the shelter guessed that he was three to four years old. He was found running loose with no collar or tags. When I met him he had been there about four days. The person who had let him run loose never bothered to claim him.

He seemed like a very sweet creature who, with a little training and love, would have made a great pet. My first instinct was to take him myself! But I already live with four dogs. Besides, I learned a long time ago that as much as I'd like to, I can't save the dog world. Millions of unwanted dogs die in animal shelters in the United States every year.

But I believe that each of us who own dogs can make a difference—even a small one. How? We should spay and neuter our pets, do a little obedience training so they're under control, and don't let them run loose. If every dog owner were a *responsible* dog owner, we could do a lot to overcome this sad situation. And of course, donations of money, supplies, or your time can help animal shelters cope with the endless supply of homeless animals they care for. Most of them do a really good job with very few resources.

If you *are* looking for a pet, check out your local animal shelter. Maybe the responsible owner for that cute little mutt sitting in a cage is you!

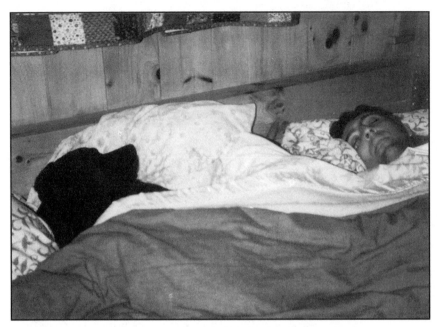

This isn't the first time I've been caught on camera sleeping with one of my dogs. Byron and I have put in a lot of cozy hours together over the past twelve years.

There's a Dog in My Bed

DEAR DOG TALK: I have a year-and-a-half-old black Lab. I've allowed her to sleep on my bed since she was a small puppy because that was the easiest way to keep her quiet at night. Now she weighs sixty-five pounds and takes up my whole bed. I know that you should never allow a puppy to do something that you don't want them to do as an adult, but I did. Now I can't get a good night's sleep. Is there anything I can do?

DEAR SLEEPLESS IN WHEREVER: Boy, you don't know how bad I wanted to say, "You should never allow a puppy to do something that you do not want them to do as an adult." But you already know that! So here is what I suggest you do so that you can have your bed to yourself.

Buy your dog a nice dog bed, or "nest," from a pet supply store or catalog source, such as L. L. Bean or Orvis. Put it right next to your own bed. Teach your dog the exercise "down-stay" and practice this exercise with your dog every day.

When you go to bed at night, tell your dog, "On your nest" (or whatever command you choose to mean that she should get on her bed). Then bring your dog to the nest, get her on it, and have her lie down and stay. If she starts to get off her nest, growl *"Nhaa!"* and make her get back on the nest. If she jumps on the bed, tell her "Off!" and haul her off your bed and put her back on her nest. Each time you put her on her nest, repeat the command, "On your nest."

This procedure can take up to a few weeks or longer before she gets the message and you finally break the habit of her sleeping on your bed. However, it will be worth it in the long run. You must be persistent and consistent if you wish to succeed. Do not cave in when she looks at you like you are the *meanest* "dog mom" who ever lived. Believe it or not, she will learn to love her nest.

If all of this seems like too much work, call your favorite department store and order a king-sized bed. That's what my wife, Barbara, Byron, our twelve-year-old black Lab, and I have!

P.S. To update this answer, I must admit that it's now our baby daughter, Hannah, who cuddles in our king-size bed. Byron sleeps comfortably on his dog nest (or sometimes on the living room couch).

A New Baby on the Way

DEAR DOG TALK: My husband and I have a two-year-old Airedale, whom we love. In November we are expecting our first child. How do we break the news to Lucy, and what can we do to accustom her to the new baby?

DEAR PARENTS-TO-BE: Congratulations! As you may know from the dedication page in *Puppy Preschool,* my wife, Barbara, and I had a child in July of 1995. It's a great experience, and I hope you enjoy it. It is, however, a big adjustment and a change in life for everyone, including the family dog.

I broke the news about the impending arrival of our daughter, Hannah, to our three adult dogs when we brought my springer pup, Crea, home from the breeder. As I held her in my hands for all of them to sniff, I told them, "Boys, I've got good news and I've got bad news." After they each took a turn checking her out and looked at me with an expression that seemed to say, "You've got to be kidding! You don't seriously plan to keep this thing!" I told them, *"This* is the good news!"

Once Hannah arrived, we did not do anything very complex to get our dogs accustomed to her. It was suggested to us that before Barbara and Hannah came home from the hospital, I should bring one of the baby's blankets for the dogs to sniff. I did not do this, but it's not a bad idea and could only help the dog become familiar with the baby.

I've read dog-training articles that suggest that Mom and Dad should get a doll several months before their baby is born and go through the motions of child care. This is supposed to accustom the dog to the new routine and let her adapt to not being the center of attention. (We did not do this, either.)

I felt very confident that our dogs would adapt well to a new individ-

The little queen and her furry court! My four dogs—Drifter, Crea, Byron, and Bentley—all adore my daughter, Hannah. The arrival of a new baby doesn't have to mean that dogs are suddenly exiled from family life.

ual joining our pack and to the changes in their lives. That's partly because our dogs have traveled with us quite a bit. They also have lived in many different places and have learned to adapt to a variety of changes. Most important, however, is that although they are indulged, they each know that Barbara and I are in charge. Having the dog (or dogs) under control before a baby comes into the home is imperative in any family.

We did let each of the dogs sniff Hannah as Barbara held her the day she came home from the hospital. Because Crea is young and exuberant, I put Crea's training collar and leash on her while she checked the baby out. During most of Hannah's first year, the dogs have not paid much attention to her (except at mealtime when they hang out near her high chair for dropped crackers or other tidbits).

However, we never, *ever* leave any of the dogs alone with the baby—not even for a second. This is our golden rule. And because of Crea's exuberance, she is not allowed in the same room with Hannah unless the baby is in her crib or in her bassinet on our dining room table. I don't want to take the chance that she might jump up on one of us as the baby is being fed or held. Crea is a puppy who is in the process of being trained. Until she is, we are taking no chances. There will be plenty of time for Hannah and Crea to interact directly when they both are older.

Another thing our dogs had to adjust to was living exclusively on the first level of our home. This helps us keep the upstairs free of dog hair, fleas, and ticks. We put up retractable baby gates at the bottom of the stairs and in several of our doorways so that we can control the environment of each room. The dogs quickly got used to the baby gates and have accepted this change very well. Again, the fact that Barbara and I have been in charge from the start is the underlying reason for our success.

If Lucy does not fully understand who the pack leader is in your household, get to work with her obedience training. Although your baby will bring many changes to your pet's routine, it will be important for you to provide Lucy with some continuity and a feeling of stability. Find some activity that you or your husband can continue to do with Lucy every day after the baby comes. A daily hike in the woods, a swim in the pond, a twenty-five-minute obedience practice session—or all three—will reassure Lucy that her entire world has not turned upside down.

On Canine Thinking and Memory

DEAR DOG TALK: Do dogs think? Do they have memories?

DEAR PHILOSOPHER: These are two very profound questions. Entire books have been written on the subject! Let me see if I can give you two simplistic answers. Yes, I believe dogs can think. I do not believe that they can reason on the level that humans can. But I believe they have limited reasoning power. Here are some examples.

I've seen my dogs get off their beds, go over to the basket of dog toys, and rummage through it until they find one specific toy. I believe that while they were on their beds they *thought* about which toy they wanted, then selected it. Or perhaps they considered which toy they wanted while they were rummaging through the basket. Either way, these actions require thought.

I've also seen my dogs make decisions. Drifter and I will be in my yard when a bunny pokes his head out of the woods. Drifter sometimes will start to chase the bunny but then look at me and decide, "I guess I'd better not; Dad won't like it." But sometimes he decides, "The heck with Dad. I *love* chasing bunnies!" and off he goes. But he always thinks about it.

Dogs have *great* memories. If they could not remember anything, they could never be trained. All dogs repeat (or avoid) behaviors based on the consequences of their past experience. This process is simple. If a behavior results in a pleasant experience, the dog will do it again. If the experience is unpleasant and the dog did not fulfill his motivation for doing the behavior, he will eventually avoid doing the behavior.

If Your Dog Is Attacked

DEAR DOG TALK: What should you do when an aggressive un-leashed dog approaches and yours is on the leash?

I have an older male Lab mix that was attacked one night as we walked down my street. I immediately did everything I could to pull the attacker off my dog. When I finally did, my dog had several tooth marks in his skull, and I had a huge hole in my jeans and gravel burns on my knees.

If my dog were attacked again, what would be the best thing for me to do? I know this is a hard question with a lot of "ifs," but I think it might be helpful to have a logical plan of action just in case. What do you suggest? Should I carry an air horn? A chemical to spray in the eyes? I hate to think I have to be armed to walk my dog!

DEAR PROTECTOR: Raising the end of my leash toward the dog in a threatening manner and growling, "No! Get away from my dog before I beat your brains in," seems to work well for me! Most dogs will back off if you confront them in a dominant manner. However, some dogs are brazen enough to keep on coming.

Unfortunately, I do not have a foolproof formula for breaking up a dog fight. Water is often effective, but a garden hose or a bucket of water is not always close at hand. I must caution you that getting in the middle of a dog fight can be very dangerous. A bird-dog trainer I knew many years ago received one of the worst dog bites I've ever seen, trying to break up a fight between his own two female English pointers.

Very often dog fights look and sound worse than they actually are. Normally, one dog quickly submits and the fight is over. Your instinct probably is to try breaking up the fight immediately, but you may be bet-ter off to let it run its course for a few seconds—even though a few seconds may seem like an eternity. You can shout and make a lot of noise, yelling at the dogs to break it up. Keep in mind that reaching in to pull the dogs apart is extremely dangerous. Chances are good that you're going to get bit. However, you may choose to take that risk if you feel your pet's life is truly threatened.

Also, keep in mind that every owner's physical capabilities are differ-ent and so is every set of circumstances. I have four dogs. Where I might let Drifter, my Australian shepherd, and Bentley, my yellow Lab, defend themselves, chances are that I would come to the aid of my puppy, Crea, and my old Lab, Byron, a lot sooner. While I feel it is our responsibility to protect our pets and family members, I certainly don't want any owners getting hurt. What I may be capable of doing, you may not. You truly have to use your own intuition under the circumstances—and please be careful!

As far as your question about airhorns and chemical sprays, I have no experience with either. Certainly I wouldn't criticize you for doing whatever you need to do to be safe. I do agree, however, that it's a sad state of affairs when we have to arm ourselves to protect ourselves from both human and canine thugs.

P.S. And don't forget to call your local animal control officer about any dog you encounter running loose.

Playing Fetch by the Rules

D EAR DOG TALK: My dog loves to play "fetch the tennis ball." The problem is that she won't give the ball back to me. She runs by me, shaking it in her mouth. When she does come to me, she clamps down on the ball, making it difficult to take the ball from her. Eventually she brings it to me because she likes to play fetch. Unfortunately, I waste a lot of time trying to get the ball, and she takes the fun out of the game for me. Is there any way to train her to give the ball to me immediately?

D EAR NO-TENNIS-ELBOW: Yes! I call it the two-tennis-ball technique. Play your game of fetch using two tennis balls. Throw one tennis ball as you give the command "Fetch!" As your dog is racing back toward you, show her the second tennis ball. She will probably become interested in the second ball and come to you. Tell her to sit. She may simply drop the first ball, anticipating that you are going to throw the ball that's in your hand.

If she does not drop the ball, take it from her mouth as you say, "Give." If she resists as you try to take the ball, try this technique: With

Fetch! Dogs love to hold and carry objects, but bringing them back to you sometimes takes a little training. Penny, a Golden retriever, has a special retrieving skill—working on her seashell collection.

your left hand, gently grasp the top of your dog's muzzle. Using your pointer finger and thumb, apply slight pressure behind your dog's two top canine teeth. (The canine teeth are the large "fangs" on either side of your dog's jaw.) This pressure will cause your dog's jaw to pop open. This handy technique is also used by veterinarians and vet techs when they need to give a pill to a cat or dog.

Be sure to always say "Give" as you take the ball. Eventually your dog will learn the command "Give" and will release things to you when you tell her to.

One last bit of advice on this subject. Never play tug-of-war with your dog with any object. Tug-of-war will only encourage her to resist releasing objects to you. Instead, the two-tennis-ball technique almost always works.

Strangers Petting Your Dog

DEAR DOG TALK: I take my dog, Kelly, into town on a regular basis. Sometimes I practice her obedience lessons, other times she does a down and stay while I read the newspaper. Kelly is a very friendly four-year-old Golden retriever that loves everyone. She is very popular, and people are always asking if they can pet her. I always tell people that it's okay to pet her, and I make her sit and stay so that she does not jump up.

My problem is that many people do not ask first. They just come up and start petting her. I've had little kids run right up to her and hug her. I don't want to appear to be a grump, but this really bothers me. What would happen if Kelly wasn't so friendly? What if, like many dogs, she was not tolerant of children? Personally, I would not bring a dog that was not friendly into a crowded downtown area, but I know that some people would. Isn't it proper protocol for people to ask first to pet a dog? Would I be wrong to suggest this to people who just run up to my dog?

DEAR GOOD MANNERS: I agree with you that people should always ask first before they pet someone's dog. Parents especially should teach their children this rule. Not only is it good manners, but it's important for the child's safety.

I often have had the same experience as you describe while working with one of my clients' dogs or my own dogs in town. I always make a point of thanking those folks, particularly the children, who do ask if they can pet my dog. I've resisted the urge to chastise those people who do not ask first. I'm not saying you would be wrong for trying to educate these ill-bred individuals. However, in a busy downtown area you may find the process a tiresome task.

Another experience I've had that you did not mention is the fellow dog owner who feels compelled to allow his dog to drag him over to my dog. The dog then has to jump all over my dog, undermining one of my training goals. I train dogs to "mind their own business." This means to ignore other dogs unless both handlers *mutually* decide that they want their pets to interact. A dog who gets all revved up every time it spots another canine is not, in my opinion, under control. Although I've kept my cool and have not blasted these well-intended but rude dog owners, I think my demeanor shows that I'm not thrilled.

Keep in mind that good manners are frequently lacking in a busy town—and not just in reference to dogs. People also let their dogs defecate on the streets, and, despite leash laws, I still see dummies walking in town with their dogs off leash. I guess the bottom line when it comes to proper puppy protocol and good canine manners is that some people have them— and others do not!

Toilet Drinking

DEAR DOG TALK: Why does my dog drink out of the toilet?

DEAR FLUSHED: Dogs don't have the same aversion to germs and odors that people do. They eat and drink a lot of things that we find unpleasant or downright disgusting. Toilet-drinking can be one of them.

But look at it from the dog's point of view: Water in the toilet bowl is cold. It's fresh (following a flush). It's at dog-level for a great many dogs. And it's available. If it really bothers you, there's an easy solution: Put the lid down!

Breeds and Breeding

The Australian Shepherd, an Unfamiliar Breed

DEAR DOG TALK: I have an Australian shepherd like your dog Drifter. I don't know much about the breed. Is there an Australian shepherd club or any other way I can learn more about the breed?

DEAR AUSSIE OWNER: You have your hands full! Australian shepherds are energetic, smart dogs. I advise lots of exercise and activities to keep your Aussie's active mind occupied. (Can you buy your Aussie a herd of sheep? Only kidding!)

The Australian Shepherd Club of America, Inc., can give you plenty of information. There is also a wonderful book on the breed, *All About Aussies,* by Jeanne Joy Hartnagle. Published by Alpine Publications, Inc., in Loveland, Colorado, it first came out in 1985 and sold for $22. In the past couple of years, the Australian shepherd has become an American Kennel Club–recognized breed. Possibly the American Kennel Club in New York City can provide you with additional information.

Ways to Find Dog Breeders

DEAR DOG TALK: What is the best way to locate a good dog breeder?

DEAR PUPPY HUNTER: First, I would ask your veterinarian. Vets often have breeders as clients. The veterinarian probably has insight into the breeder's credentials and the quality of dogs the breeder produces. If your vet doesn't have a client who is breeding the type of dog you are looking for, call other veterinary offices in the area.

If you meet someone who owns the breed you are interested in (and you like their dog), ask where they got it. Also, find out if they were happy dealing with their breeder.

That's my independent Aussie, Drifter. He's also one of the smartest dogs I've ever known.

The American Kennel Club (AKC) offers a breeder referral list that you may find helpful. The woman I spoke with on the phone at the AKC assured me that the breeders on their list have been checked out and are qualified breeders. However, unless I had firsthand information about a particular breeder, I would definitely ask the breeder for a list of references. The address for requesting this AKC breeder list is 5508 Centerview Drive, Raleigh, NC 27606. The phone number is 1-900-407-7877.

The Curly-Coated Retriever, a Very Unfamiliar Breed

DEAR DOG TALK: Do you know anything about curly-coated retrievers?

DEAR CURLY: Not much, as they are very uncommon. A few summers ago I was invited to a client's home for a party. One of the guests was visiting from Maryland with his two dogs, Pepper and Dover. Dover was a curly-coated retriever, a breed which—at the time—I had never met before. This beautiful black dog weighed between fifty and sixty pounds. Her body was covered with short, tight black curls that required no grooming and did not shed much. She was a friendly and animated dog who radiated intelligence. This breed carries the blood of the Irish water spaniel, the Labrador, and the poodle. They are noted for their excellent ability to retrieve waterfowl and are said to have a soft mouth, which means they don't crush or maul the birds while carrying them. *Mmmm,* duck season is coming up.

Surprise! It's a Pet-Shop Puppy

DEAR DOG TALK: I would like to surprise my mother, who lives alone, with a miniature poodle puppy for Christmas. I can't find a breeder with puppies and have been warned to avoid pet shops. Are pet shops as bad as I've been told?

DEAR CHRISTMAS SPIRIT: I'll be glad to answer your question about pet stores, but I feel compelled to comment on the first sentence of your letter. A puppy is the worst surprise gift in the world. Unless your mother is physically and mentally able (and willing) to deal with the all-encompassing responsibility of raising a puppy, you're not doing her a

A physically and mentally sound dog is more important than "dog show" good looks. Wally, a fox terrier, has both!

favor. Even people who choose to raise a puppy can feel overwhelmed by the amount of work involved.

Unless your mom lives in a warm-weather state, the end of December is a horrible time of the year to try to housebreak a puppy. Puppies need to be taken out on an average of every thirty minutes in order to form the important habit of eliminating outdoors. This is not fun in zero-degree temperatures surrounded by ice and snow!

As far as pet stores go, I don't know what you have been told, but I do not recommend that anyone buy a dog from a pet store. Reputable dog breeders do not sell their puppies to pet stores. As a result, pet stores are forced to buy puppies from less than wonderful breeders or from production-line puppy mills.

A responsible breeder will not sell a puppy to an inappropriate owner. Pet stores, on the other hand, do not screen owners. Anyone with the right amount of cash can purchase a puppy from a pet store. Also, it's important that puppies stay with their littermate brothers and sisters and mother until they join their new human family. This doesn't happen with pet store puppies. The puppies sit in a cage for twenty-four hours at a time, often for days or weeks until they are purchased. This is not at all conducive to good canine mental health. It also makes housebreaking difficult, if not impossible.

Veterinarians regularly see pet store puppies with health problems. Along with the genetic problems related to poor breeding, pet store puppies are often exposed to many contagious diseases. There is nothing sad-

Two cute girls! Alyssa, age six, poses with Carrie, a Keeshond, during a summer afternoon. Dogs and children seem to go together like peanut butter and jelly.

der than becoming attached to a sweet, innocent, vulnerable puppy only to watch him suffer with illness.

Despite all of the negatives, I still meet some pet store puppies every year who turn out to be great dogs. This is only because dogs are resilient creatures who sometimes make it through the worst circumstances. However, it's a risk I would not take.

If you still think your mother is a good candidate for owning a dog and you know for sure she would really like one, my best advice is to surprise her with a nice book about miniature poodles (and a copy of *Puppy Preschool!*). That way she can read about this breed and make an informed decision about the realities of raising a puppy. Then, after the holidays, you can help her find a good breeder, wait for a litter of pups to be born, and perhaps help her buy some of the supplies she will need, such as a crate, food bowl, leash, collar, etc.

Spay and Neuter Laws

DEAR DOG TALK: There are a couple of questions I would like to ask you regarding the spaying and neutering of dogs and cats. I am wondering if you know of anybody, for instance a humane society or an organization, who is putting together a law that requires pet owners to spay or neuter their dogs and cats. What are your thoughts and ideas about spaying and neutering domestic pets? Do you wish there was such a law?

DEAR RESPONSIBLE DOG OWNER: I am not aware of any organizations that are lobbying local, state, or federal legislators to pass a law to force pet owners to spay or neuter their dogs and cats. However, it is possible that such efforts are being made somewhere in the country.

As far as my own feelings, I advocate that every cat or dog who is not going to be bred *responsibly* be spayed or neutered. At the very least, responsible breeding entails searching the pedigree lines of *both* parents for health defects, paying for health screenings of *both* parents to determine if they have sound hips, eyes, etc., paying *every* medical bill associated with complications of the birth, placing *all* the puppies in loving homes with owners who agree not to breed them, and being prepared to take *any* puppies back if they develop health problems or don't fit in well with their new family. It takes a lot of work and dedication to be a responsible breeder, but most people can't be bothered. That's why more than ten *million* unwanted cats and dogs are killed in the United States every year. Overbreeding, in my opinion, is a real crime.

A vast majority of veterinarians believe that spayed and neutered pets live longer, healthier lives. Unspayed female dogs and cats are susceptible to a condition called pyometra, which is an infection of the uterus. There is also a high incidence of breast tumors in unspayed female dogs. Unneutered male dogs often suffer from infected prostate glands and cancerous anal growths. I also believe that with many intact male dogs, sexual frustration is a factor in their behavioral problems.

Despite the fact that I have such strong views on the subject of spaying and neutering, I would not support a law that required it. I feel this way for a couple of reasons. One, I don't care for Big Brotherism. I may be idealistic and naive, but I hope people will someday become educated and choose to do the right thing.

Two, who would determine which dogs and cats should be bred and which should not? I personally would not want the world to be made up exclusively of purebred dogs—whose reason for having been bred is to appear in some silly dog show. Some of my favorite dogs are the mixed breeds who come through my classes every year. A ban on breeding might be a law that the bureaucrats would love, but I believe it would be much too complicated to regulate.

Hunting Skills in a Pet

DEAR DOG TALK: I thought I would be able to do a little bird hunting with our three-year-old springer spaniel. But she didn't seem too interested. I think she liked the ride in my truck better than anything else! I thought springers were supposed to be hunting dogs.

DEAR BIRDLESS: The root of your problem may be that your dog does not come from hunting, or "field," lines. As various breeds have become popular as family pets, many breeders no longer try to maintain the breed's original instincts through selective breeding. This is true of hunting dogs as well as working dogs, herding dogs, terriers, and hounds. As a result, there are a lot of dogs out there who are terrific pets but wouldn't know how to herd a flock of sheep, kill a rodent, track a rabbit, or, in your case, flush a bird. That's not necessarily a terrible thing, since most dog owners today don't need these jobs done. But it can be an obstacle if you are looking for an occasional hunting outing with your dog.

My springer spaniel, Crea, comes from field stock and is terrific at finding birds. (She is also a great family pet and an excellent "demo dog" in my obedience classes.) But she doesn't look like most springers that you see, because none of her ancestors were bred for dog show competitions. They were all bred strictly for hunting skills and, after many generations, this practice produced a slightly different looking dog.

When told what kind of dog she is, many people responded with, "Really? I have a springer (or my friend has a springer), and they don't look very much like your pup."

Well, that's because Crea is a field-bred springer spaniel. In the excellent book *Hup: Training Flushing Spaniels the American Way,* author James B. Spencer profiles the different dog breeds that are used to flush game birds. In his excellent chapter on springers, "The English Springer Spaniel—A Popular Pair," he points out that the American Kennel Club recognizes the field-bred and show-bred English springer spaniels as one

This is Remi, a springer spaniel specially bred for field work. He's great at finding pheasants, but he's also an all-around terrific family dog.

breed. However, they are so distinctly different in everything from appearance to working ability that they could be two distinct breeds!

This may not make you feel any better about your springer's abilities. But don't give up after one try. Keep hiking together in areas where pheasants may live. She may start responding to those interesting bird smells. And if not, you still got some exercise and had a great outing together. Not a bad combination!

Springer Rage Syndrome

DEAR DOG TALK: I know that you own an English springer spaniel. I'm thinking about getting one for a bird dog and a family pet. Someone I was talking to about the breed told me that they can be mean. They mentioned Springer Rage Syndrome. Do you know anything about this and how it can be avoided?

DEAR RAGING: I'm not an expert on the subject of Springer Rage Syndrome, but I'll tell you what I've learned. From what I understand, Springer Rage Syndrome is a genetic fault that causes an epileptic-type seizure. However, instead of having a seizure in the traditional sense, the dog violently attacks whomever it is near. This "seizure" can last from several seconds to several minutes. Then the dog snaps out of it and acts as though it has no clue of what happened. Obviously, rage can be a very dangerous disorder.

Conventional obedience training is not going to help a dog with rage syndrome. It's possible that a veterinary canine behaviorist could prescribe a drug that could help some of these unfortunate dogs. However, this is a genetic problems that can only be eliminated through careful selective breeding.

From my research on the English springer spaniel breed, I learned that there has never been a documented case of rage syndrome in the field-bred variety of springers. So I told the breeders that I interviewed, "I don't want a puppy whose ancestors have ever driven within a hundred miles of a dog show!" This was not only to avoid rage syndrome but because I, too, wanted a serious bird dog. (Springers from show stock will make mediocre

Visitors at my house had better like dogs! Uncle Karl is treated to an affectionate morning greeting from Bentley, Drifter, and Byron. Now, if Karl could only figure out how to move his arms and get out of bed.

bird dogs at best.) If you want a purebred pup that you can turn into a great dog, you have to start with good breeding. A well-bred dog is worth the extra money.

Nonallergic Breeds

DEAR DOG TALK: We are thinking about getting a family dog. The only problem is that my eight-year-old son, Parker, is allergic to dog

Cairn terriers are one of several breeds that people with allergies can usually live with comfortably. Lola doesn't shed, and she's a happy, tail-wagging individual—even in the snow.

fur. His allergist told us that a nonshedding breed would be all right. Could you suggest some breeds that do not shed?

D EAR ALLERGIC: Poodles, one of my favorite breeds, do not shed, and they come in three size varieties. They're also smart, loyal, and lovable. Wheaten terriers and cairn terriers also do not shed. Wheatens are medium-sized with a long coat, and they're very sweet. Cairns are small and fiesty. The most famous cairn terrier is Toto in the movie *The Wizard of Oz.* One of Drifter's best friends is a cairn named Sammy DiMargo. Sammy is extremely bright and well-trained.

These breeds are just a few of the nonshedders. Go to the library or buy an all-breed dog book. They're fun to look through and also have a lot of helpful information. Study the breed descriptions, and I'm sure you'll find the right breed for you and your family.

Good Handling and Training Tips

Sending the Dog Off for Training

DEAR DOG TALK: We are planning to get a black Labrador retriever puppy in a few months. Would we be better off taking our dog to obedience school, hiring a private trainer to come to our house, or sending our dog off for three weeks to stay with a trainer to be trained?

DEAR FUTURE PUPPY OWNERS: Sending a dog "off to be trained" is my *least* recommended of your three options. That's because I'm a strong advocate of teaching people how to train their own dogs. I believe that dogs respond well only to whoever trains them.

Contrary to what some people think, a dog is not like a computer. When a computer is programmed, it doesn't matter who operates it. Anyone who hits key "A" will get the same response on the screen.

A dog, on the other hand, is a living creature with a brain. When you train a dog, what you essentially are doing is developing a relationship and a form of communication between you and the dog. This relationship cannot be handed over to another person.

When a dog is sent off to a kennel to be trained, consider how much time the dog is actually being trained—and how much time he is sitting in a kennel run. When a person takes one of my obedience courses and learns to train his dog, I suggest that he spend about forty-five minutes a day practicing the exercises. Even if a trainer at a kennel works with your dog *two hours* a day, what is your dog doing for the other twenty-two hours? He's sitting in a kennel run being socially isolated. This is certainly not helping the dog adapt to the rules and routines of your household.

In addition, for the twenty-five years that I've been involved with dog training, I've never met a dog who spent three weeks at a kennel and came back responding to his owners anywhere near the way he responded to the trainer. I strongly recommend that you enroll your dog *and* yourself in an obedience course designed to teach *you* how to do the training.

Should you work with a private trainer or attend group training classes? There are benefits to both formats. Group training classes are great for socialization, especially for puppies. Dogs get to meet other dogs and people and have a special night out. Group classes are also less expensive than hiring a private trainer.

Some people mistakenly believe that group classes are better because they think "it's good to train a dog with distractions." This would be like saying that if you wanted to learn to read French, you should blast rock music as you studied—so that you could read French and listen to loud music at the same time! In reality, the music would distract you so that you wouldn't be able to learn.

Ideally, you should study French in a quiet environment where you can concentrate and absorb the information. As you became proficient with the language you could then play the radio at a low volume. When you were fluent in French, you could blast the music as loud as you wished and still be able to comprehend what you were reading.

The same holds true when training a dog. You want to teach him in an environment that's conducive to learning. A group class has too many distractions for a dog to learn new behaviors in the class. In fact, a well-designed group class should not be designed to train the dog. It should be designed to teach the owners training techniques. Then the owners go home to train their dogs. (Of course, the dogs attend class so their owners can try the techniques with them.) Only after the dog has learned a training exercise should the owner introduce distractions to the training environment.

You certainly cannot expect to receive as much individual attention in a group class as you would from a private trainer. Group training classes often have from eight to twelve dogs attending. Owners and dogs must come to the class when it's in session. If you miss a class, the course continues on without you. With private instruction, however, the trainer usually comes to your home. The course schedule is more flexible so the trainer can accommodate your busy schedule. Plus, the trainer gets to meet your family, see the layout of your yard and home, and observe the dog in his own environment. This helps personalize the instruction to you and your dog. It also makes problem-solving easier because the trainer can see where and exactly how the problems take place.

Joshua, a German shepherd–Siberian husky mix, is a sweet, beautifully trained dog. His owner did it all herself without a lot of expense. Anyone with a little time, a good training program, and the commitment to do it can have the same results.

The bottom line with either format of instruction is that you have to practice with your dog a bit every day. Your dog is not going to become well-trained if you do not work with him, even if you are spending more money on a private trainer. Whether you let your new puppy become an out-of-control monster or you teach him to be a sweet, well-behaved adult is ultimately up to you.

Training Dogs for Their Owners

DEAR DOG TALK: I have a question about your approach to training. I've read your book *Dog Talk,* and I love your "Dog Talk" newspaper column. I got the impression that you did not train dogs for people but taught people how to train their dogs. Then I read in one of your recent columns that you are offering a three-week program of training dogs for owners. Why the switch in philosophy, and does training dogs to listen to other people work or not?

DEAR TRAINING PHILOSOPHER: I still believe that the ideal approach to training a dog is to teach the owner how to do it—and to have the owner work with the dog every day. My traditional course is just that—a five-lesson, step-by-step training program. However, I've found that some people are not able to start working with their dogs right away. Owners call me and say, "I'm taking a month-long vacation" or "We have a new baby in the house" or "I'm hectic at work right now." "If you can get my dog started, I'll work with him every day when my schedule loosens up to reinforce the training."

If the owner is sincere, he can get good results with this approach. However, if the owner is looking for a "John Ross magic-wand solution," he's out of luck. Training a dog is not like programming a computer! With a computer, all you have to do is hit a specific key to get a specific response. Anyone who hits that key will get the same response. Dogs, however, are living creatures with a brain. When you train a dog you develop a relationship and a form of communication between yourself and the dog. And dogs learn quickly who they have to respond to and who they do not.

When I train a dog for its owner, I work with the dog five days a week for three weeks. The dog continues to live with the owner—I simply pick the dog up and work with him for an hour each day. I generally start the dog in a relatively distraction-free area and eventually end up working the dog in town with lots of distractions. The objective of this three-week program is simply for the dog to learn each of the obedience exercises. When I have the dog doing the exercises correctly, it is then imperative that the owner join me for several sessions and learn how to handle the dog properly. The owner must still practice with the dog every day, turning the new behaviors into deep-seated habits.

This program is almost like a jump-start on training. I can take most dogs and get them to the same point in three weeks that it would take novice handlers between five and ten weeks to achieve. This is partly because performing the training techniques correctly is second nature to me, which makes learning faster and easier for the dog.

Also, after training dogs for close to twenty-five years, I've developed the intuition to know when I can move on to the next step in training or, with some dogs, skip a step entirely. This is another reason I get dogs doing the exercises quicker than most owners can. However, I cannot develop deep-seated habits with a dog in just three weeks. That takes time. Owners must take over and continue the training if they are serious about success.

Too Impatient to Train a Dog?

DEAR DOG TALK: I have a six-month-old puppy. She is a mixed Lab and collie. She needs to be trained, and several people (including my veterinarian) have told me that I should be the one to train her. My problem is that I'm not sure I have the patience to train a dog. Is there an alternative?

DEAR IMPATIENT: There are always alternatives, such as having someone else train your dog for you. However, in my experience I've found that dogs only listen well to the people who train them. Some dogs respond *only* to the person who trains them. So I have to agree with the advice you have received. Learn how to train your dog and work with her yourself.

As far as patience is concerned, it's true that patience is a virtue—especially when it comes to dog training. However, most people are not born with a world of patience. Luckily it's a trait that can be developed. Keep in mind that if you don't have the patience to train your dog, you're certainly not going to have the patience to put up with an *un*trained dog.

When I think of someone losing their patience with a dog, I imagine them getting frustrated and hitting, choking, or doing some other abusive thing to their poor animal. Maybe that's not what you mean. Many people confuse not having patience with a lack of perseverance. It takes time to train a dog. Dogs learn by consistently repeating behaviors. So the trainer must make working with the dog a priority in life. Behaviors must be repeated every day until good habits are formed. This requires perseverance on the part of the trainer.

Also, dogs only follow direction from individuals they view as the pack leader. A person does not have to be overbearing, rough, or harsh to become a pack leader. But that person must have the ability to take charge and be assertive. Consistency is also a pack leader quality.

Get involved with a training class that offers a step-by-step program. A step-by-step approach makes it easy to be successful with your dog right from the start. I've found that success is truly the best motivator in dog training. The more you succeed, the more you want to keep working with your dog. The ability to follow directions from the trainer is also important for success.

While it is true that not everyone is capable of training a dog, most people can do it if they make a valid effort. Keep in mind that if it were simple, everyone would have a well-trained dog—and many people don't. If you really don't think you can train your dog, you shouldn't own one, in my opinion. Maybe you should get an aquarium!

Abusing the Kennel Crate

DEAR DOG TALK: I know that many dog trainers and vets recommend using a cage for housebreaking and controlling a puppy. But the way I've seen some of my friends use the cage makes me think it's a bad idea. They leave their puppy in the cage all day while they are at work and then when the puppy is wild in the evening, they put him in again to keep him out of their hair. Are they abusing the cage or the puppy? Or am I just out of touch with proper training?

DEAR IN-TOUCH: Your observations are exactly right. These own-ers are using their crate (cage) completely wrong. The crate is a useful and essential tool for teaching housebreaking—but only when it's used cor-rectly. It's also a place to put the pup when you can't supervise him. It's most definitely not a substitute for all the things the puppy needs from his owners—attention, play, cuddling, and supervision.

The puppy should be confined to its crate no more than four hours at a time during the day. During the night, when the pup's asleep, it can be about twice that long. That means that if the owners work full-time, they must come home at lunchtime (or arrange for someone else to do so) and let the puppy out. He'll need to empty his bladder and/or bowels, drink some water, eat lunch (if he's still eating three meals a day), and run around a bit to stretch his legs. Then he can spend the afternoon back in the crate.

When the family comes home in the evening, they must make the puppy a priority. They should play with him, walk him, train him. Being away from a puppy all day and then ignoring him all evening is a good combination for having a poor relationship with a dog. The dog will prob-ably never be trained if the owners choose to spend so little time interact-ing with him.

At the moment, I have a three-month-old springer spaniel puppy, named Crea. Barbara and I are crate-training Crea, and she's doing really well. (We actually have two crates—one upstairs in our bedroom for nighttime use and the other in the living/dining area.) A few old towels in the crate give her a soft bed. Pillows or dog beds are not recommended at this age because puppies love to chew them to shreds.

When Barbara and I are busy in the office or leave the house, Crea goes into her crate for a few hours. That way she can't wander around the house chewing things or have a housebreaking accident. When we arrive home, the first thing we do is take her outside to eliminate. Then she can have some supervised freedom in the house. She can play with her toys, have a drink of water, wrestle with our other dogs, or explore the downstairs while we clean up the kitchen, do laundry, or read the mail. Because we're supervising her, she learns what she may do and what's off-limits.

Sometimes the crate serves as the canine equivalent of a toddler's "time out." Crea certainly has her wild, out-of-control moments when she's torturing our old Lab, Byron, or grabbing everything out of the laun-dry basket, or persistently trying to pull at the tablecloth in the dining room. Even when she's tired after a hike, she'll have these moments. That's when we know she needs to be crated to help her settle down. Eventually she'll be mature enough to settle herself and lie down on the floor for a nap. (She has never once done that on her own—yet!) Until then, the crate helps us structure her life and teach her the behaviors she needs to know to be a calm, well-behaved adult dog.

Older Dog Meets Puppy

DEAR DOG TALK: I have a four-year-old mutt. He's always gotten along good with other dogs. Last week I got a little friend for him. She's an eight-week-old female Lab/chow mix. I thought he would be thrilled, but he hates her! She tries to play with him, but he growls at her. All he wants to do is lie in the corner and sulk. Is there anything I can do?

DEAR TWO-DOG OWNER: Chances are good that your adult dog will adjust and learn to accept—and maybe even love—your new puppy. I know firsthand what you're going through. The members of my canine pack, which consists of Byron the black Lab, Bentley the yellow Lab, and Drifter the Australian shepherd, were totally bummed out when I got my springer spaniel puppy, Crea. In fact, Drifter, who is a renowned puppy-hater, sulked with a downright evil look on his dog face. Bentley growled every time Crea looked at him, and Byron would just look at me with an expression that seemed to say, "When is she going home? Tomorrow, right?"

My wife, Barbara, and I were very careful to supervise interactions between the puppy and the adult dogs. We didn't want the adults to hurt the puppy, and we didn't want the puppy to constantly torment the adults. But we never separated them, except when the puppy went into her crate. Time together was important for them to get to know each other. We took them for hikes together so that the older dogs would associate the puppy with fun. Our outdoor adventures in the moors and on the beach were a natural way for us to feel like we were all part of one pack.

Also, we were careful to maintain our positions as pack leaders. From a canine point of view, a new member of a household is disruptive to the pack. In the wild, it's a time when the hierarchy can potentially change. The pack leader may be challenged, or there may be fights as pack members test each other to establish a new position. Certainly, a new puppy is in no position to challenge adult dogs, but there can be tension, nevertheless, because of the change. Keep this in mind as you interact with your dogs: Don't "feel sorry" for the older dog and let him walk all over you. Certainly give him individual attention, but maintain your image as the pack leader. In the long run, it will keep your pack stable and will help both dogs adjust to the change more quickly.

It took about a month in my household before everyone adjusted to Crea's arrival. Now Drifter loves Crea. He plays with her every single day. They wrestle and chew on each other. If she becomes a little too aggressive, he nips her with just the right amount of force to put her in her place. Byron does not enjoy being chewed on, so he'll get a dog toy and play tug-of-war with her. Bentley still grumbles a little, but Crea now licks him all over the mouth when he does this. He just wags his tail. (I think Bentley is not willing to admit it yet, but he likes her, too!)

My advice is to do the same kinds of things with your two dogs. Supervise when they are together so that both adult and pup don't aggravate each other. Do lots of fun activities with the two of them, especially activities where there is no chance for competition. For example, go on dog hikes as often as possible. Don't throw one tennis ball for the two dogs. You want to encourage them to feel like a team, not to be rivals. And give it a little time. They will soon accept the fact that they are members of the same pack, and before long they'll probably be good friends.

This happy crew of Malteses (Tuffy, Dolly, Fluffy, and Dixie) ranges in age from three to ten. Older dogs and puppies can learn to get along fine as long as they are supervised and each is given some separate space and attention.

Tied Outside All Day

DEAR DOG TALK: I don't want to start trouble, but I have a neighbor who leaves his poor golden retriever tied up outside twenty-four hours a day. Although this situation always disturbs me, I am particularly upset when the weather turns cold. Isn't this cruelty to animals? Is there anything that can be done about it?

DEAR CONCERNED NEIGHBOR: I'm not sure if there is an easy solution to helping this dog. I would suggest that you contact the police and speak with the animal control officer. If tying a dog outside legally is not considered cruelty to animals, I think it should be. It's certainly a sad existence for any creature, let alone a canine who is so dependent on social interaction. Goldens, as a breed, usually thrive on the relationships they develop with their owners. In my opinion, living alone in the backyard is a form of emotional cruelty to a dog.

Tying dogs up is a bad practice for other reasons. Dogs become frustrated by the isolation, and this frustration often manifests itself in behaviors such as excessive barking, self-mutilation, and aggression—to name a few. When people find that their only alternatives are to socially exile a dog to the backyard or to let them run loose, they should consider *not* owning a dog. Goldfish—not golden retrievers—make nice pets, too!

Exercise is so important to dogs—especially to athletic breeds such as Labrador retrievers. Bentley shows off his Frisbee-catching skills during a hike on the beach.

How to Flunk Obedience Class

DEAR DOG TALK: I have a new dog and am thinking about taking an obedience class with him. A friend of mine took a class recently, but she and her dog flunked out. I'm worried that this will happen to me and my dog! Do you have any advice before I enroll?

DEAR A-STUDENT: The fact that you are motivated to succeed is an important step in the right direction. Also, you will find that with a well-taught class, dogs don't "flunk out"—only owners do! It's an extremely rare situation to get a dog who is truly untrainable. Unfortunately, it's not as rare to get owners who are unteachable.

In the many years that I've been involved with obedience training, I have found that there are some common denominators among owners who don't have success with training. In fact, I list these points in a handout I give to all my students. If you can eliminate these flaws from your training, you are bound to succeed. I call it the Ten Point Failure System.

1. Failure to practice every day.

An important requirement for dogs to develop a conditioned response is repetition. Dogs rarely learn anything with one experience. You must practice, practice, practice.

2. Failure to adapt to the training program.

Inexperienced dog owners train haphazardly. Experienced trainers develop a structured, logical, step-by-step training program and adhere to it. Stick with the instructor's program. Do not skip steps.

3. Failure to perform training techniques as designed.

Successful end results are only achieved if training techniques are performed correctly. Imagine taking golf or tennis lessons. What would happen if the pro showed you a specific procedure and you did it 30 percent the pro's way and 70 percent your way? Chances are great that you would not achieve the desired results. This is very true with dog training. It is your responsibility to carry techniques out precisely as they are designed.

Failure to obtain the recommended training equipment will also hamper your success. Imagine taking ice skating lessons on roller-skates. You certainly won't get very far. You won't get very far in dog training either if you don't use the proper equipment.

4. Failure to adapt obedience exercises to everyday living.

Obedience exercises are not parlor tricks. They are designed to serve as control mechanisms. Use them in everyday life. While walking your dog, make him sit and stay while a neighbor jogs by. When eating dinner, have your dog do a down-stay. These are just two examples. All of the exercises in my courses have specific, practical uses. It is important that dog owners apply them in their appropriate context.

5. Failure to close your mouth and open your mind.

It is an amazing and frustrating ordeal for experienced obedience instructors to deal with self-professed know-it-alls. Whenever obedience instructors attempt to enlighten these individuals with facts and advice, they are contradicted. The instructors' facts and advice have been gathered through years of research and practical experience. The know-it-alls' experiences are based on the untrained dogs they have lived with or known in the past. Do you want to learn something? Close your mouth and listen!

6. Failure to fulfill your dog's need for physical activity.

All dogs are different. They have been bred for different, specific purposes. Some high-energy breeds can never succeed with training if they are pent up with energy. My first dog was Jason, an Irish setter. I attribute 50 percent of my training success with Jason to exercise. A daily one-hour run channeled his exuberance. This gave Jason the ability to settle down and concentrate during our training sessions.

7. Failure to match your training approach to your dog.

A dog and a handler are a team. Team members have to work smoothly together in order to succeed. Team members must be compatible with each other. If you have a submissive dog and come on with a heavy macho approach, training will not progress smoothly. If you have a dominant dog and you are an unassertive old softy, you are doomed to failure.

Often complete mismatches in physical strength do not do well.

Every dog obedience instructor has had the sweet little old lady with the 110-pound rottweiler in class. It is your responsibility to choose a dog that you can effectively handle and train.

8. Failure to view the world through a canine point of view.

Dogs cannot think or act like humans. But most humans can think and act like a dog. Handlers who develop the ability to do this will communicate effectively with their dogs. Dogs who are labeled stupid or stubborn during training often are just confused. Guess who is confusing them—you! It is your job as the trainer to learn "dog talk."

9. Failure in the dog obedience class setting.

There are certain traits that I see in handlers who fail group dog obedience classes. Missing classes is a trait that spells failure. If the course you are enrolled in is a structured, step-by-step program, it is imperative to attend all sessions.

Another failure trait is chronic lateness. Week after week, this student wanders into class late. Besides disrupting the rest of the group, the student misses valuable information. It's ironic because this student is usually the one who needs the information the most.

An annoying trait to the instructor is inattentiveness during class. These students spend time in side conversations or allow their dogs to pester the dogs next to them. It's disrespectful to any teacher to disrupt a class. Granted, it is the responsibility of the instructor to maintain order in class. But it's also the responsibility of the student to pay attention and conform to the class rules.

10. Failure to maintain your dog's physical health.

Dogs who are physically unsound will not respond well to training. A dog with hip dysplasia may be in pain when sitting. If your dog seems to be uncomfortable in the hind end, have him examined by your veterinarian. Your dog should always have vaccinations updated. Be sure your dog does not have intestinal parasites such as tapeworm, roundworm, hookworms, or whip worms. Have fecal samples checked at least twice a year. Check your dog's ears for infections. A yearly physical is mandatory.

Routine grooming is also important. Be sure that your dog's toenails are trimmed to the proper length. A matted coat will inhibit your dog's performance of exercises. Check under your dog's legs and behind his ears. Matts in these places can be bothersome to a dog.

Neutering the male dog is advisable for many reasons. Intact males can be aggressive, mark territory, and ignore commands when seeking females. Training such dogs can be highly frustrating. Neutering can help.

Other Factors

I've listed the ten most common ways that people fail when training their dogs. If you can eliminate these ten problems, your odds for success will increase greatly. However, you should be aware of some other reasons for failure. If you are working with a dog obedience instructor, be sure that this person is competent. Obedience instructors cannot effectively teach what they do not know. Without proper experience they are incapable of developing an effective training program for you.

A physical limitation or disability may inhibit some handlers from being successful. For example, being extremely overweight or physically too weak may contribute to failure. A person may simply be too old or infirm to succeed with the demands of training a dog. I've also met individuals who were just too unintelligent or uncoordinated to train a dog.

However, my rule is to never underestimate the individual handler. I competed in obedience trials against a young woman in a wheelchair. Her disability didn't prevent her from having wonderfully trained dogs and winning her share of first-place ribbons. I've also had people succeed in my classes who were every shape, size, and age. I'm personally not the smartest or most coordinated person in the world, but I have had many years of dog-training success. With determination, commitment, and hard work, you can, too.

Training for Bird Hunting

D EAR DOG TALK: I want to train my one-year-old dog to be a good hunter, but she doesn't seem to get the idea of carrying birds back to me. You would think for a retriever she would do that best. I'm thinking of sending her off to a hunting expert for training, but I have mixed feelings about this. Will she learn better from him or should I persevere on my own?

DEAR BIRD DOGGER: I recently attended a two-day hunting seminar for spaniels and retrievers, which gave me some insight into what "hunting experts" do. I had the misfortune of watching the "expert trainers" demonstrate a technique they called the "nerve toe pinch." We were told that this procedure would teach a forced retrieve and also teach the dog that we (its owners) were "alpha dog."

Here's how this technique works. You put the dog on a training table (similar to a picnic table) with a metal pole attached vertically to one end. You tether the dog to the pole by his neck as tightly as possible. You then take a piece of string and tie it around the dog's left front leg just above the ankle joint. You run the string down the front of the dog's leg and tie a slip knot around the dog's two middle toes. From the toes you let out about ten or twelve inches of string and then wrap the string around a stick to give yourself a handle.

You hold the stick handle in your right hand and hold another stick (the retriever stick) in front of the dog's muzzle. Then *as hard as you can,* you pull down and out on the handle attached to the string. When the dog screams and cries out in pain, you place the retriever stick in his mouth and release the pressure on the dog's toes. After three or four repetitions, most dogs learn to quickly grab the retriever stick to relieve the pain.

The next step is to hold the stick in front of the dog's mouth and give a command to grab the stick. If he does not respond immediately, you again inflict pain to the dog's foot. I saw this done to three springers and a black Lab. One of the springers was only seven months old, like my pup Crea. The other three dogs were not much older. The Lab flipped out so badly that he never grabbed the stick. He screamed in pain and fought until he broke loose from the pole. It was one of the most pathetic sights I've ever seen. His owners simply stood there and watched.

I was the only participant at the seminar who works professionally with dogs. For the past twenty-three years I've taught dog owners how to train their dogs to be well-behaved family pets. Anyone who has read my book *Dog Talk* knows that I am not a "give-'em-a-cookie-and-never-tell-'em-no" dog trainer. However, I *never* use training techniques that cause dogs to shake like a leaf and scream out in agony. Watching this abuse affected me far greater emotionally than I even realized at the time.

Being involved with dogs for so long, I have seen abuse take place in other trainers' obedience classes. I'm always amazed by dummy dog owners who allow the trainers to abuse their pets. Owners will stand by and let the "expert" half choke their puppies to death, simply because the dog failed to stay or to comply with some other command. Unfortunately, inexperienced owners put their faith in the "expert." Wake up, people! Protect your dogs when you see abuse. It doesn't take any dog experience to recognize when an animal is panicked and in pain.

Unfortunately, there are many trainers who are more than willing to use abusive techniques. They exploit the dogs with abusive handling to achieve their own personal goals, boost their own egos, and further their reputations as "champion" dog trainers.

I lived with a wonderful German shorthaired pointer for fifteen years. For eleven of those years we hunted birds together. I plan to do the same with my new springer pup. However, I'd hang up my shotgun in a second and keep her only as a house pet before I'd ever abuse her. Some of these so-called experts might know a lot about training techniques, but they don't know a single thing about dogs.

So that's my answer. Unless you can find a hunting-dog trainer who will use techniques that are fair and nonabusive, I recommend reading a few good hunting books, collecting advice from experienced friends, and doing it yourself. You have a decade ahead of you of good hunting, so what's the rush? Plus, I can attest that nothing beats the satisfaction and bonding that are achieved by training your own dog and then together bringing in those birds.

Do's and Don'ts with a New Dog

D EAR DOG TALK : I've never owned a dog before, but my husband and the kids really want to get one. We know training is important but don't even know where to begin. Can you give us some basic training tips?

D EAR FAMILY : Here's a list of ten do's and don'ts to post on your refrigerator. If you and everyone in your family follows these rules, you will be way ahead of most other dog owners—even before you start obedience class.

1. Do supervise a puppy at all times to prevent housebreaking accidents and unwanted chewing. Do provide a structured environment

for your puppy, such as a kennel crate, when you can't supervise or are not at home.

2. Do be consistent with your dog. Clear household rules help your dog know what you expect from him. Dogs understand "Always" or "Never." They do not understand "Sometimes."

3. Do train him to obey your commands by first *showing* him how to respond. Shouting or yelling commands will not help your dog understand what you want.

4. Do provide plenty of exercise. Tired dogs are good dogs.

5. Do use natural corrections when necessary, such as a growl-like *"Nhaa!"* or a shake on the scruff of the neck. Hitting or kicking dogs only teaches them not to trust you.

6. Don't ever scold your dog after the fact upon finding a housebreaking accident or a chewed item. Effective corrections are given *as the behavior is happening.* Ten seconds later—or longer—is too late.

A new dog can bring a lot of changes to a household. Starting out right can make the next twelve to fifteen years wonderful.

7. Don't shout your dog's name as a correction or he will learn to ignore hearing his name.

8. Don't call your dog to you to give a correction or he will never want to come when called.

9. Don't let your dog do anything as a puppy that you don't want him to do as an adult. That's because dogs are creatures of habit, so try to form good behavior patterns right from the beginning.

10. Don't forget to love your dog and give him some attention each day. He will return it a hundredfold!

Timing Is Everything

DEAR DOG TALK: I have a seven-month-old Pekingese that is very stubborn. He is not totally house-trained and will sometimes chew items in the house that are not his. He knows when he is bad. All I have to do is walk into the room and he cowers and hides. When I show him the mess and scold him, he acts remorseful, but he'll do it again a few days later. Does he have a poor memory? Am I being too soft? Should I increase the discipline? I'd hate to have to hit him, but I'm getting frustrated.

DEAR FRUSTRATED: Your Pekingese puppy is not stubborn, he is confused. And guess who's confusing him? You are! The reason he is confused and continues these unwanted behaviors is because the timing of your corrections is off.

Proper timing is essential when teaching a dog to avoid any unwanted behavior. Your correction has to happen precisely as the dog is doing the unwanted behavior. Even better would be a correction that comes as the dog is *thinking* about doing the unwanted behavior! Ten seconds after the fact is too late to teach the dog to avoid the behavior.

Here is a classic example of what I'm talking about. When my springer spaniel, Crea, was four months old, she licked the porcelain handle on the woodstove in my living room. It was very hot and she burned her tongue. She yipped in pain. She has never gone near the stove again! However, had the timing been off, she would not have learned to avoid the stove. Imagine if she licked the stove handle and felt nothing. If she then walked upstairs to my bedroom, looked at the rocking chair and *then* felt the burning sensation, she would think that the rocking chair caused her discomfort. If the timing of the disagreeable experience continued to be off, she would continue to lick the stove, never learning that it was something she should avoid. This would not indicate a stubborn dog, it would indicate a confused dog.

The demeanor that you are interpreting as remorseful is actually apprehension. Your puppy doesn't have a conscience like a human does, but he does have a great memory. He remembers that whenever you enter the room and there is a housebreaking mess or a chewed item on the floor, he has the disagreeable experience of being scolded.

What he—and all canines—cannot do is project thought into the future. As he is making the mess, it feels good, so it's okay to do. He has no way of understanding that in two minutes or two hours or two days he will be in trouble.

Increasing discipline is not the answer, either. Hitting your puppy will only ruin your relationship with him. It will not stop these unwanted behaviors. You will stop the behaviors only with supervision and well-timed corrections. A gutteral *"Nhaa!"* is sufficient discipline for most dogs. Say it precisely as your puppy is thinking about doing (or is in the act of doing) the unwanted behavior. This will help him understand what you want.

Keep in mind that you cannot time corrections properly if you are not keeping an eye on your pup at all times. At seven months old, your puppy should never be out of your sight unless he's in his crate or a comparable structured environment. A gutteral growl ("*Nhaa!*"), consistency, and good timing are the keys to a well-trained dog.

What Is Your Dog Thinking?

DEAR DOG TALK: In one of your past columns you talked about the importance of timing a correction when training a dog. The fact that you must correct the dog precisely as he is doing the unwanted deed (as opposed to later) made a lot of sense to me. What confused me was the statement you made that "even better would be a correction that comes as the dog is thinking about doing the unwanted behavior." My question is, how does one know what a dog is thinking? Are you suggesting mental telepathy with dogs?

DEAR MIND READER: No, I'm not suggesting mental telepathy. I *am* encouraging you to learn to read your dog. "Reading a dog" is a skill that experienced dog trainers take great pride in being able to do. And believe it or not, it's not a hard thing to learn. Fortunately for us, dogs are extremely open and honest animals. Everything they are thinking is practically written all over their faces.

Sometimes it is obvious what the dog is thinking. When you leave your sandwich sitting on the living room coffee table and you see your dog looking at it and drooling, you can be sure he is thinking about grabbing it. That would be the best time to growl *"Nhaa!"*

At other times the signs are not so overt. My old Aussie, Drifter, is a notorious puppy biter. He will never look for trouble or go out of his way to bite an exuberant, adolescent canine. However, if one crowds his space he will give the pup a quick nip. His physical demeanor just before he does this is very subtle. He does not growl. The fur on his back does not go up. He simply strikes like a barracuda! After many years of close observation,

What is *this* dog thinking? Mookie, a black Labrador retriever mix, is known to think a lot about food and car rides. What this expression means is anyone's guess.

I discovered that just before the strike, his eyes shift and flicker. When I see the eyes flicker, I growl *"Nhaa!"* and that aborts his attack. I'm correcting him when he is *thinking* about it.

Certainly the more experience a person has interacting with and training dogs, the more proficient they will become at reading dogs. In turn, their timing for corrections will improve, and they will see that the dogs they are training will become better trained faster.

In reality, the majority of people who come through my training programs are pet owners with a minimal amount of dog experience. I urge these students to trust their intuition. If you think that your dog is *thinking* about doing an unwanted behavior, growl *"Nhaa!"* Ninety-nine percent of the time you will be right! For the one percent of the time that you may be wrong, you are better off wrong with a correction than late with one. That's because, again, good timing is essential for effective training.

My Dog Ignores My Husband!

DEAR DOG TALK: I've trained my year-old chocolate Lab using your book *Dog Talk.* Although she is still an excitable puppy, she listens to me pretty good. She does not listen at all to my husband and constantly mouths him and jumps on him. She doesn't act this way with me because she knows that she will not get away with it.

My husband never had dogs growing up and is a pushover with our Lab. He is also very busy with his business and doesn't have time to work with her. Is there any way I can get her to listen better to him? If I can't do it, do you have any suggestions on how I can motivate my husband to work with our dog?

DEAR PUSHOVER'S WIFE: I have found that dogs only respond well to commands that come from the people who train them. They never respond as well to commands from other people. Some dogs will not respond *at all* to commands given to them from others.

Don't mistake a dog for a computer. When you use a computer, all you have to do is touch a specific key to get a specific response. Everyone who hits that key will get exactly the same response. A dog, however, is a living creature with a brain. Obedience training develops a *relationship* as well as a form of communication between the dog and the trainer.

If you come to your husband's rescue by correcting your dog every time she pushes him around, she may learn to leave him alone when you are present. But when you are not there, chances are great that she will take advantage of him. Ideally, he should establish himself as a dominant pack member in the eyes of your dog. This simply requires being firm with the dog (not rough or cruel), plus spending a few minutes every day training her.

Unfortunately, we don't live in an ideal world. If people are not motivated, you cannot badger them into training a dog. When having a well-behaved dog is a priority, people do find the time to work with their dogs a little bit every day. That's not easy, though. If it were, everyone would have well-trained dogs!

"Rubbing a Dog's Nose in It"

DEAR DOG TALK: I have a three-month-old yellow Lab puppy who sometimes has housebreaking accidents. My boss at work suggested that I "rub his nose in it." I don't have a tremendous amount of experience training dogs, but my intuition tells me that there has to be a better way. Please tell me there is! I don't think I could bring myself to do that to him.

DEAR INTUITIVE: Well, I always urge people to trust their intuition, and yours is right on the money. Rubbing a dog's nose in its excrement is both unnecessary and disgusting.

First of all, when a puppy has a housebreaking accident, it is not the pup's fault, it's the owner's fault. Puppies do not instinctively know where we want them to go. It's the owner's responsibility to supervise the puppy at all times and to make sure that the pup is outside when he needs to eliminate. When an owner cannot supervise, the puppy should be in a structured environment, such as a kennel crate.

It is all right to correct your puppy if he has an accident indoors, but *only* if you catch him as he is about to go or in the process of eliminating. Ten seconds after he has gone is too late! He will never learn anything from an untimely correction.

If you do catch your puppy having an accident, your correction should be a guttural growl: *"Nhaa!"* A well-timed growl will clearly give your puppy the message. Overcorrections, such as hitting the pup or putting his nose in it, will not speed up the teaching process or make the training more effective. They *will* confuse your puppy and make him distrust you. The key to successful housebreaking is supervision and the appropriate use of a kennel crate.

Are Pet Tricks Stupid?

D EAR DOG TALK: Do you think it's okay to teach dogs tricks? My friend thinks it's cruel and stupid, but I think it's fun.

D EAR TRICKY: Tricks that are safe can be a lot of fun for both you and your dog. In fact, working together to learn them is a form of training but without the pressure that tricks *must* be mastered (unlike basic obedience, which is essential for a well-behaved dog). Tricks are strictly for fun and amusement—and some extra cookie rewards for your pup. Don't train like a drill sergeant, and if your dog doesn't seem inclined to learn a certain trick, drop it. Forcing the issue is stressful and *can* make the experience cruel and stupid.

But let a well-seasoned pro give you a bit of advice. Never, I repeat, never show off with your dog! I'll never forget the night that Barbara and I invited two dear friends to our house for dinner. I decided that they had to see the new "stupid pet trick" that I had taught to my sixteen-month-old springer spaniel, Crea.

The trick goes like this: I tell Crea to sit and stay. I then reach into my pocket and pull out a dime. I drop the dime on the floor while Crea re-

Rowing a boat is *not* one of Cork's tricks! But this Irish water spaniel is great at finding deer antlers shed after mating season. Tricks or clever behaviors that are safe and humane can be a lot of fun for dogs to learn.

mains sitting. I tell Crea, "Fetch!" and she retrieves the dime off the floor. (If you think about how thin a dime is, that's pretty good work.) Then Crea comes over and sits in front of me with the dime in her mouth. When I hold out my hand and command "Give," Super-Spaniel drops the dime into my hand.

Well, it all went perfectly up to the point where she drops the dime into my hand. When I commanded "Drop," Crea went *"gulp"* and swallowed the dime! Everyone roared. Boy, did I feel like a dope. I had to listen to an hour of one-liners about my wonder dog and my great trick-training abilities. I tried to recover my dignity by attempting to convince my friends that this was all part of the trick—and that if they came back the same time the next night, Crea would poop out fifty cents! But no one was buying it. Let me repeat, never show off with your dog!

Behavioral Problems

Destructive Chewing

DEAR DOG TALK: Help! My six-month-old springer spaniel is destroying my house. He was pretty good at first and would only chew things once in a while. This was usually when we were not home. Then, about a month ago, he started chewing the rug when we weren't looking. We put away the rug, but he still chews something whenever he's left alone.

DEAR CHEWED UP: Puppies generally chew things when their owners leave them alone because they feel abandoned by their pack members (you and your family). Chewing is a way to release frustration. Also, teething increases the urge to chew. At four months old, puppies begin to lose their milk teeth as adult teeth grow in. They begin to chew more vigorously than they did before, especially as the adult teeth settle into the jaw. The combination of these factors creates a house-destroying fur-ball!

Because chewing is normal for dogs, the answer is not to *stop* chewing but to condition the dog to chew only the proper things. Dog toys, nylon bones, and rawhide are examples of acceptable chewing items.

To condition your puppy to chew these items, you must supervise him closely. If he chews something other than his toys, correct him as soon as he grabs a forbidden object. You do *not* need to hit him. Simply growl *"Nhaa!"* Correcting *after* you find a destroyed object is too late! A dog will certainly act frightened or submissive if you correct him after the fact, but he will not associate your correction with the chewed item. In other words,

Providing appropriate chew items is an important part of training a puppy. Bentley, an adult Labrador retriever, has a solid habit of chewing only on his toys because that's all he was allowed to do as a puppy.

he won't learn to stop chewing your valuable stuff. Proper timing is *everything* in dog training.

After you correct your puppy, remove him from the area where he was chewing. Then provide him with his acceptable chew toy.

When you cannot supervise your puppy, you must provide him with a structured environment such as a kennel crate. Put some of his chew toys in the crate with him. When he's in the crate he will have two options. He can curl up and go to sleep or he can chew on his own toys. Those are the behaviors you want him to practice over and over again—until they are solid habits. Be sure to use your crate properly. Dogs should never be crated during the day for more than four hours at a time.

At around a year old, teething is finished and the puppy has learned he's not being deserted whenever you leave him. If you have followed these guidelines, your puppy will be trained not to destroy the house when left alone. He will simply do what he's been doing all along—curl up and go to sleep or chew on his own toys.

On the other hand, if you allow your puppy to destroy things on a regular basis, destructive chewing will become a habit, and he'll chew whenever he's left alone. That's because dogs form habits (good or bad) by repeating behaviors. It's time to put a stop to destructive chewing today!

Food Thievery

DEAR DOG TALK: I have a nine-month-old neutered male German shorthaired pointer. He's a very good puppy, but he's the world's biggest food thief. He puts his front feet up on the counters or kitchen table and grabs food. I feed him twice a day, and he's not a skinny dog. Why is my pointer always so hungry, and how do I stop him from being a thief?

DEAR POINTER PARENTS: First off, you don't own the biggest food thief in the world. Yours is a rookie. *I* own the biggest food thief in the world! He's my eight-year-old Australian shepherd, Drifter. As a matter of fact, I playfully tell people that Drifter is only half Australian shepherd—his mother was a state park raccoon!

In his day, Drifter has eaten an entire Boston cream pie. He did this in about thirty seconds, while standing in the middle of the dining room table. Once while visiting my grandmother, he ate an entire box of her prunes—cardboard box and all! All we found was the lid.

In my briefcase I carry doggie biscuits to use with my training classes. He loves to raid that bag and steal all the treats. He also has stolen countless loaves of bread, rolls, and beagles (I mean bagels).

Once after a dinner out, my wife, Barbara, brought home a portion of a meal that she could not finish. Her plan was to have beef kabobs for lunch the next day. Even though the "doggie bag" was far back on the kitchen counter, Drifter had beef kabobs as an evening snack that night.

One day a few years back, after just filling our storage barrel with forty pounds of fresh dog kibble, I took a short sailboat cruise around the lake we lived on. I was gone about an hour. I returned to find Drifter with his head in the tipped-over barrel, grazing away. He had eaten about twenty-five pounds of dog food, and his sides were grossly distended. I truly thought he would die of bloat, a dangerous stomach ailment. I quickly rushed him to our veterinarian, who advised "no food" for three days and also to limit water for a day or two. I'm convinced that Drifter would have eaten every last morsel had I not walked in when I did.

These stories are just the highlights of Drifter's eight-year food-stealing career. As you can see, your nine-month-old rookie has a long way to go before earning that coveted title of "World's Biggest Food Thief"! However, don't despair. Here are several things that I did with Drifter that should help you.

Drifter made his first food-snatching attempt when he was around six months old. He did it right in front of me. I growled *"Nhaa!"* as soon as his front feet touched the kitchen table, and he quickly scooted away. By six months old, Drifter clearly understood that *"Nhaa!"* meant he did something wrong and to stop immediately. He may have tried again once or twice, but in a short time Drifter learned never to steal food—when I was looking!

Unfortunately, when no one was watching, Drifter would still steal food. On my weekly radio program, "Dog Talk," I interviewed a well-known dog trainer, the late Job Michael Evans. In one of his books, Job taught his readers how to entrap their sneaky mutts as the dog was doing an unwanted deed and thought that no one was watching. This is what he suggested I do: Put a bowl of chips on the coffee table in the living room, ignoring Drifter as I do so, and leave the room. Make footstep noises as I walk upstairs but quickly tiptoe back down. Ever so sneakily, peek around the corner and watch Drifter. When he gets his nose in that bowl, charge at him as I growl "NOOOO." Grab him by the scruff of the neck and give a firm shake as I tell him in a stern voice, "Don't you ever touch those again!"

I did this precisely as instructed. Drifter fell for it hook, line, and sinker. What did Drifter learn? Now he comes and checks around all corners before he steals food!

I tried a motion detector that made a loud disturbing noise when moved. After fifteen seconds of this racket it shuts off and resets itself. I put a muffin on the edge of the dining room table and sat down to watch a football game. After a few minutes, out of the corner of my eye I saw Drifter edging toward the table. As his front feet touched the table I growled *"Nhaa!"* as the motion detector went off. "Stay away from there!" I yelled. Drifter slunk away, with a dejected look on his face. The motion detector shut off and reset itself.

The phone rang in my office, and I ran upstairs to answer it. I talked for about ten minutes, then came down and got back into the game. About an hour later I looked over at the table. *The muffin was gone.* Drifter had struck again. He obviously was not going to be deterred by a mindless motion detector.

So what's the answer? You can and should try all the techniques that I described here. Although they didn't work with the World's Biggest Food Thief, they may work with your dog. Plus you must do what I do: supervise, supervise, and supervise. I've trained myself *never* to leave food where Drifter might get it. I constantly check countertops, tabletops, pantry doors, and trash cans. When I do slip up, I blame myself (or my wife).

Drifter's food-stealing antics have brought him some notoriety, but I'm not sure they can compare to something that a presidential dog once did at the White House. I read a great anecdote that a dog owned by President Franklin D. Roosevelt once snuck into the White House kitchen when no one was looking. What did he find? The contents of nineteen breakfast platters that were about to be served. And, of course, he helped himself to the contents of each one! Obviously a presidential kitchen is no different from yours or mine—at least from a dog's point of view.

Why is your dog always so hungry even though he's not underfed? I believe it's because in the wild, canines are gorgers. This means they eat as much food as they can—because they don't know when the next meal will come. Many of our domestic dogs have retrained this trait. It makes your job of controlling your dog's access to food that much more important.

One final suggestion: Train your dog to lie down and stay. He can't beg at the table or jump up on it if he's doing a down-stay. Good luck! I hope your dog doesn't steal his way to Drifter's infamous title.

P.S. (four months later): Drifter has struck again. There's another notch in the collar of the world's greatest food thief. Last week my good friend "Debbie the Groomer," her boyfriend Darren, and her wonderful shepherd/husky mix, Joshua, came for a visit. They were not in the house ten minutes when Drifter snuck into the guest bedroom, opened the zipper on Debbie's duffel bag (he didn't rip anything—he *opened* the zipper!), and ate Joshua's food. When we found Drifter with the torn, open plastic bag that held the food, we growled *"Nhaa!"* at him in a harsh tone. Drifter looked guilty and sorry, but later in the evening he thought his antics were really funny. He sat there with a big smile on his dog face as I told the story to some friends.

Begging for Food

DEAR DOG TALK: I have a one-year-old black Labrador retriever. How do I stop her from begging when we eat? My husband and I have never given her human food, but she's still a beggar.

DEAR HOUNDED: One of the biggest myths in dog training is that if you never feed dogs human food, they will not beg. It's rarely true. Dogs are smart, and they love food (especially Labs!). They also have a great sense of smell. Before long, every puppy is going to figure out what you're doing at the dining room table. Then they usually start to beg. Certainly if you give dogs food when they beg, you will reinforce their behavior. However, I've found that whether you give them food or not, most dogs try to beg at the table.

You can prevent begging by doing two things. First, don't reinforce the behavior by giving your dog any food from the table. (If you want to share a few human-food tidbits, you can put them in your dog's bowl after your meal is finished.) Second, train your dog to lie down and stay. This is the obedience exercise called "down-stay." It's impossible for your dog to beg at the table if she is doing a down-stay several feet away from the table.

Down-stay is an important control mechanism. During a down-stay, the dog lies down in the place you choose and does not leave that spot until you release her. I remember one dinner party that Barbara McKinney and I threw. There were *seven* dogs in the room. Each of them did a down-stay throughout the meal. You wouldn't have known there was a single dog in the house!

The down-stay is not only useful during meals, it's great when you have guests over or you bring your dog to someone else's home. The dog can lie down in the room with everyone without being a nuisance. In fact, down-stay is useful any time you want your dog under complete control. It is also a great technique to convince your dog that you are her pack leader.

Before you can use this obedience exercise to control begging while you eat dinner, you must first teach it to your dog in a setting where you can give her your undivided attention. Briefly, this is what's involved. (For complete instructions, see my training book *Dog Talk*.) First, choose an environment with minimal distractions, such as a quiet living room. Have your dog lie down in whatever spot you choose. Draw an imaginary circle in your mind around your dog. She must remain lying down, although she can move her head and wag her tail. She can even shift her position, such as flopping on her side or rolling belly up. Those movements are fine. But do not let her stand up, do "G.I. Joe crawls" across the floor, or roll out of the imaginary circle. If she tries these things, put her back in position *every time.*

Start off doing this for only fifteen or thirty seconds. When that's successful, try for a full minute. By slowly increasing the time of each down-stay, you'll soon have a dog that can lie down and be under control in many different settings. As I said, down-stay is a great control mechanism. If my dog knew only one thing, it would be this exercise.

Afraid of the Kennel Crate

DEAR DOG TALK: I have a male boxer who is fifteen months old. He is a lovable, good dog, but we can't leave him home alone. He destroys things. He's already broken closet doors, chewed molding, ripped my couch, and clawed through Sheetrock. Need I go on?

We've basically adjusted our lifestyle to accommodate Strider, which I feel is ridiculous. We have tried keeping him in a kennel crate when we're not home, but he's petrified of it. As soon as we'd put him in the cage, which was a struggle, he would drool or foam at the mouth and shake terribly. He developed colitis from it. He even tried to pry his way out and wound up cutting his mouth! Needless to say, we got rid of the cage.

So now my husband works nights and I work days, and Strider is never left alone. Is there any other way around this? Do you think training would help? My husband seems to think that no trainer can guarantee that a dog will be good when left alone.

DEAR BOXED IN: It's true, there are no guarantees when it comes to behavior—canine or human. But dogs can be predictable once habits form. And habits form simply by repeating behaviors. Every time Strider destroys something when you are not home, he is reinforcing this destructive behavior. Every time this behavior is repeated, the more deep-seated the habit becomes.

Dogs normally chew things the first year of their lives as they go through the teething process. Chewing also is a frustration release. When we leave a puppy alone—even for a short time—the puppy feels abandoned. He doesn't yet understand that we will return, so to release frustration he chews something.

Because chewing is a normal behavior, we do not try to *eliminate* chewing. Instead, we want to redirect the behavior so the puppy learns to chew acceptable items, such as rawhide, nylon bones, or sterilized natural bones (available in pet supply stores).

This is accomplished in two equally important ways: supervising the puppy when we are home and providing a structured environment when we are not home. When left alone in a structured environment, the puppy has two options: curl up and go to sleep or chew on his own toys. If the puppy does this every time he is left alone during the first year of his life, it will develop into a good, solid habit. That's your goal with Strider too, even though he is now fifteen months old.

Your dilemma is that Strider will not allow you to use a structured environment (the crate) without having a wingding! First, keep in mind that you are in charge—not the dog. Also, a structured environment does not have to be a crate. You could build a pen in the basement, use a laundry room, or an area blocked-off with baby gates. However, a crate is an ideal structured environment because there are no posts, walls, or gates to chew.

I do not know what Strider's aversion to the crate is. You said he is "petrified" of the crate. Assuming that he has never had a bad experience with the crate, I think he may just be associating the crate with separation from his pack (you and your family).

If Strider were my dog, I would convince him that when he was crated he should go to sleep or chew his own toys. This is partly accomplished with obedience training. By training Strider, you will develop a pack leader image. Once you accomplish this, *all* of your interactions with your dog will be easier. In training, I would put emphasis on the commands "Lie down" and "Stay." I also would teach Strider to stop doing any unwanted behavior immediately when I growled *"Nhaa!"*

I would start to use the crate again, but for short sessions *when I was home.* If Strider started to claw at the crate or carry on, I would growl *"Nhaa!"* and make him lie down. When he was behaving in the crate, I would reward him with praise and a dog biscuit. After a week of successful "crate practice," I would leave the room for thirty seconds. If Strider remains quiet, I'd give him a food reward and also lots of praise. If he starts to carry on, correct him. Continue to increase the time in short intervals as he does well. Eventually, start leaving the house for short periods (no more than a minute) until you can do it for longer periods. Each time you return, praise and reward Strider for his good behavior.

To help Strider overcome his crate aversion, switch the type of crate you are using (plastic airline crate versus metal wire crate). Put the crate in the kitchen or family room so he can be near you. Feed Strider all of his meals in the crate with the door open. Drop treats into the crate so that he has to go in to get them. Be sure that when you do crate him he has a few toys and safe bones to chew on.

I would use the crate for the next two years before I allowed him to be free alone in the house. You're going to have to give at least equal time to the new behavior (curling up and going to sleep or chewing on his own toys) as the old behavior of trashing the house existed. For example, if Strider has been destroying the house for a year or more, you will need about the same amount of time to break the habit and reestablish a new behavior. So the longer you wait, the tougher your job will be. That's a good reason to start today!

Chewing on and Biting People

DEAR DOG TALK: My German shepherd puppy is constantly chewing on my children's and my arms. I know he's not being vicious and that he is just playing, but his teeth are sharp and it hurts! How can I make him stop?

DEAR CHEWED UP: You're half right, your puppy is not being vicious. However, he is not just playing, either. He is "testing." Because your puppy views your family as his pack, he is trying to find out where in the pack he stands. Chewing on you, called "mouthing," is one of the ways your puppy does this. Other ways include climbing on you, growling at you, and being possessive with toys. Some puppies are even brazen enough to snap or bite.

Puppies learn these testing behaviors at a very young age—between three weeks and eight weeks old. They need these behaviors to find their position in the hierarchy of a canine pack. If the dogs were wild canines, such as wolves, the hierarchy would be important for maintaining social harmony. In their life as domestic pets, dogs still are attuned to pack hierarchy.

Puppies learn testing behaviors by interacting with their littermate brothers and sisters and with their mother. If you have ever watched a litter of puppies, you'll see them growling, wrestling, chasing each other, and biting. It looks like play, but a lot of learning is going on at the same time.

By the time a litter is seven or eight weeks old, the puppies have learned which of their brothers and sisters they can push around and which they should respect. An experienced dog breeder can easily pick out the pecking order among the puppies.

Fortunately for us, even the most dominant puppy in the litter learned that its mother was the undisputed pack leader. When it tried chewing on mother dog's legs or ears, she growled. All of the puppies learned that this growl meant to stop whatever they were doing immediately. If a puppy ignored its mother's growl, she would escalate her aggression by snapping at the pup. I've even seen mother dogs nip puppies and make them squeal. This teaches puppies that their mother's warning growl really means business!

On the other hand, a mother dog is usually consistent and patient. And she is not unnecessarily harsh. If she has to growl at her pup sixteen different times before he finally learns to avoid chewing on her, she will. As long as the puppy stops when she growls, she will not escalate her aggression.

At around eight weeks old, puppies leave the litter and come home to live with their new human pack. The puppies use the same techniques with us to determine whom they can push around and whom they must respect. It's your job to teach your puppy that you are the new pack leader.

The quickest and most effective way to communicate with your puppy is to imitate canine behavior. When your puppy uses any of his testing behaviors on you or your family members, growl at him *"Nhaa!"* It's dog talk! You also must imitate canine behavior by being consistent with this correction. Consistent means growling *every time* the pup does an unwanted behavior. Your growl should have a low, guttural tone. Loud is not as effective as guttural. Don't wait until you are frustrated or angry to growl. You're simply using your voice as a training tool. Every time your puppy mouths, correct him with a growl.

Timing is also an important ingredient when training a dog. The ideal time to growl is when your intuition tells you that your puppy is *about* to do one of the testing behaviors. The next best time is as he is doing it. Ten seconds after he has done it is too late to correct. Watch him closely!

If your children are under ten years old, they are not old enough to convince a puppy that they are dominant pack members. In this case it is the responsibility of the adults in the family to supervise interaction between children and the puppy. Adults must come to the rescue and correct the puppy when he harasses the children.

Testing behavior is not an indicator of bad temperament. However, puppies who think they are in charge can be a handful. And dogs who reach adulthood (at two years) thinking they are pack leader often have aggression problems. I suggest that you take mouthing seriously and, excuse the pun, nip it in the bud.

Charging at Strangers

DEAR DOG TALK: I have a six-month-old Border collie named Jimmi. He's a very good puppy, but in the last month he has been acting weird with people. He runs up to them barking and then runs away. He will keep doing this even if we tell him "No." If the people ignore him, he will come up to them after a while and be fine. But if they try to talk to him or pet him while he's barking at them, he'll growl and show his teeth. Is he a psycho?

DEAR PSYCHED OUT: No, he's a herding dog! Herding dogs seem to go through some strange phases during adolescence. These canine phases may include unwanted behaviors, like the ones you describe. Unfortunately, the behaviors do not go away on their own, so you must take action in order to change them. If you didn't do something to cause a change, each behavior is reinforced every time it is repeated. With enough repetition and reinforcement, the behaviors become habits.

With your situation, you first need to teach your puppy some basic obedience commands. He must learn to stop doing whatever he is doing when you growl *"Nhaa!"* The puppy also needs to learn to sit and stay and to be quiet on command. (These exercises are outlined in detail in my training book *Dog Talk.*) Then you are ready to practice the following exercise: Whenever Jimmi meets new people, you must have him on the leash. That means (at least for a while) no free runs on the beach, where he can run up and act tough with strangers. To meet people, have Jimmi sit and stay at your side. If he barks, use the "Quiet" command. If you get taken by surprise and do not have him on a leash when someone shows up, abort the unwanted behavior by growing *"Nhaa!"* and quickly getting the leash on your dog. Then put him into a sit-stay.

If Jimmi likes doggie treats, carry some in your pocket at all times. While your pup is sitting quietly at your side, give the visitor some doggie treats to offer to Jimmi. If Jimmi growls, tell him *"Nhaa!"* and have your visitor back away and ignore the dog. Continue to have a light, pleasant conversation with the visitor. Let your puppy pick up the "vibes" that everything is fine and that you do not feel threatened by this person. Be sure to keep your pup in a sit-stay. If Jimmi does take the treat from the visitor, that's great! It will help him form an agreeable, positive association with new people.

Many people unknowingly reinforce unwanted behavior by praising their dog at the wrong time. Here's an example of what I mean. Two people meet on the street. One of them has a dog. The dog looks at the other person and starts to shy away and growl. The dog's owner—in an attempt to reassure the dog and let him know that everything is all right—tells the dog in a soothing tone, "It's okay. Be a good boy. Nobody's going to hurt you."

The dog hears these praise tones (without understanding the words) as he is growling and acting shy. He feels he is being rewarded for what he is doing! The correct thing to do is to praise your pup only when he is showing signs of being friendly and outgoing. *That's* the behavior you want to encourage and reward.

Chasing Cars

DEAR DOG TALK: My Border collie loves to chase cars. I'm scared to death that she will get hit by a car. How can I stop her from doing this?

DEAR SCARED: Keep her on a leash! Border collies are dogs with a strong herding instinct. Things that move quickly such as cars, motorcycles, bicycles, and joggers will trigger the dog's chase reflex.

Dogs form habits by repeating behaviors. Every time your dog chases a car, that behavior is being reinforced. If your dog is on a leash when she lunges toward cars, you can correct her and train her to avoid doing this. To do this, you need a six-foot leash. The leash should be made of cloth or leather. You'll also need a properly fitted metal training collar. For a Border collie the training collar should have medium-sized links. When the collar is around your dog's neck, place your finger in the ring where the leash attaches and pull up gently. You should have two to three inches of excess collar. If the collar is too long or too short, it will not release properly and won't work as a training tool.

With your dog on the leash and collar, stand away from traffic on the side of the road. Keep the leash relatively loose. (Do not restrain your dog on a tight leash. Restraint teaches dogs absolutely nothing!) When a car comes by, correct your dog with your voice first, giving a firm *"Nhaa!"* Do this even if she just *looks* like she wants to chase the car. If she ignores your verbal correction and lunges toward the car, give a jerk-and-release correction on the training collar and repeat *"Nhaa!"* After you correct her, make her sit and stay. (If she is not trained to sit and stay, teach it to her *before* you try this technique.)

It may take several months before your dog learns to completely ignore cars when she is on the leash. Be patient.

Caution: Even when your dog learns to ignore cars when she's on the leash, this does not necessarily mean that she will ignore them off the leash. You *can* have control over her when she's off the leash if she stops unwanted behavior when you growl *"Nhaa!"* and responds immediately to the command "Come!" It takes work, but it's certainly possible.

Car chasing is nothing more than a game of Russian roulette played by someone you care about. If your Border collie continues to chase cars, she eventually will get hit. Please do not let this happen. Having control over your dog is the key. If she is not obedience-trained, get to work.

Aggressive Around the Car

DEAR DOG TALK: I read a newspaper story that described an "act of compassion" that almost turned to tragedy. It told how a child reached her hand through a partially opened car window to pet the dog inside. When she did this the dog nipped her. This story bothered me, because I couldn't decide who was wrong, the dog or the child. What's your opinion?

DEAR COMPASSIONATE: I'm truly thankful that this child was not seriously bitten. However, the dog's behavior does not surprise me. It is instinctive for canines to protect their territory, and many dogs become particularly protective in the confines of a car. My dog Drifter, who loves people (especially children), is obsessive about protecting my house and car.

An important rule that adults should teach their children and also follow themselves is: Never try to pet any dog that is in a parked car. Dog lovers who want to say hello to dogs they see in cars around town can greet them verbally. Don't reach in to touch them (this goes for dogs in the back of pickup trucks, too). Even dogs that you know (and that know you) may nip or bite in this situation.

Dog owners who leave their dogs in the car have a responsibility as well. Although it is important that your dog has fresh air to breathe when he is left in a parked car, don't leave the window open wide enough for the dog to get his head out. (If it's too hot this way, then leave the dog at home.) It is frightening and can be dangerous to have a dog lunging out a car window at you as you walk by the car. If you know your dog is protective of your car, park in an isolated part of a parking lot to minimize stimulation to your dog from people walking by. A little common sense on the part of dog owners and dog enthusiasts can go a long way to minimize problems.

A Shy, Biting Puppy

DEAR DOG TALK: I just bought a sheltie puppy two weeks ago. Amber was four months old when I got her. When I picked her up from the breeder's, she was outgoing, friendly, and her tail never stopped wagging. But when I got her home she completely changed. She's afraid of my husband, who is a quiet, gentle person who loves dogs. My friend from work visited yesterday with her ten-year-old daughter, and Amber hid from them. When I finally got her to come out, she snapped at the little girl when she tried to pet her!

I called the breeder and when I told him what was going on, he asked me what I did to the dog to make her act this way. We haven't done anything mean to her! I'm baffled. What did we do wrong? Help!

DEAR BAFFLED: I can't tell you how many times in the last twenty-five years I've heard this story. First of all, you didn't do anything wrong—your breeder did. He sold you a puppy at the wrong socialization period in your dog's life. The ideal age for a puppy to transfer from one pack (which was its mother, littermates, and the humans in the breeder's household) to a new pack (your family) is between seven and eight weeks old. Puppies who are sold after this period are often shy and spooky. The interesting part of this phenomenon is that in their original environment the puppies are confident and outgoing. The shyness does not manifest itself until the puppy leaves that environment.

Breeders who know little or nothing about canine behavior or about dog training naturally assume that the new owner "did something mean" to the puppy. That's usually not the case. If breeders are not able to sell a puppy at the correct time in the puppy's life, it is their responsibility to socialize the puppy. Amber's breeder should have taken her for walks in the park, exposed her to new people (including children), and even enrolled her in a Puppy Preschool class. All of these things would have prepared her for the big, scary world out there.

Luckily, the prognosis for your pup is not that bad. I've yet to meet an incorrigible four-month-old puppy! Although you may never turn Amber into an extrovert who runs up and licks new people all over the face, you can turn her into a stable individual. The worst scenario with a puppy like

Linus is a sweet but cautious little Shetland sheepdog puppy. Socialization and obedience training are making him more confident and secure. Without this training, he could become an overly shy adult who bites everything that frightens him.

Amber is letting her develop into a "fear-biter." A fear-biter is an unstable dog who panics when exposed to new people and becomes aggressive. This could possibly happen if you do not immediately begin a program of socialization and obedience training.

First, get involved with a good obedience-training program. Obedience training will do two things. It will give you control over your dog. She has to learn to stop what she is doing when you growl *"Nhaa!"* or *"No."* She also must learn to stay reliably and come when called.

In addition, obedience training will build Amber's confidence. Dogs are always most confident when they are doing something they are familiar with. For example, imagine that I met you and Amber on the street. If Amber could sit and stay at your side while we talked, she would be more confident than if she were bouncing around at the end of the leash trying to hide from me.

The second part of stabilizing your puppy is socialization. When you get some control over her through obedience training, take her everywhere with you. Take walks into town, take rides in the car together, visit the pet supply store, etc.

Let Amber meet kids and adults—as many different people as possible. However, *do not* force Amber to approach anyone or have anyone force themselves on her. That will only make Amber more fearful. Just make her stay at your side while you have a conversation with the person. The person you are greeting can talk to Amber in a soothing tone. If she shows signs of being outgoing and friendly, praise her! If she shys away, do not try to soothe her with gentle, comforting words. This is interpreted by dogs as praise and would only reinforce her shyness. If Amber likes food, have your friend offer her a tidbit. If she accepts it, praise her.

I once owned a German shorthaired pointer, named Jena, whom I got when she was six months old. At first she was extremely shy—an emotional basket case. It took me two years of effort, following the program described above, before she stabilized. But the results were worth it. Jena lived to be fifteen years old and became a relatively confident creature. I do believe that she would have been happiest if everyone but she and I (and the pheasants we hunted together) disappeared from the face of the earth! But she learned to hold her own. She learned to accept new people and situations and never got so panicked that she snapped or bit. She even earned two American Kennel Club obedience titles. It was a lot of work, but she turned into a really great dog. Yours can, too. Get started today!

A Terrier Who Barks . . . and Barks . . . and Barks

DEAR DOG TALK: I have a mixed-breed terrier who is almost one year old. She's a very good girl, but she loves to bark. Anything will set her off! Kids walking by the house, a dog in the yard, or my neighbor pulling into his driveway sends her into a frenzy of barking. How do you train a dog not to bark?

D EAR TERRIER-IZED: I don't train dogs not to bark; I teach them to be quiet on command. In other words, my dog will bark (which is natural canine behavior), but I can tell him, "Drifter, quiet!" and he will clam up.

The drawback to this approach is that you have to give the command "Quiet" every time you want the dog to stop barking. That's because dogs don't grasp the concept, "Stop barking and don't make a sound for the rest of the day." For example, if a dog comes into my yard, Drifter will bark. I command, "Drifter, quiet!" and he stops barking. Then fifteen minutes later when the UPS truck pulls in, Drifter starts barking again. Again I have to give the command, "Drifter, quiet!"

Before this will work with your dog, you have to teach her that the command "Quiet" means to stop barking. The command "Quiet" will be meaningless to your dog if you just yell the word at her. In order to help your dog form an understanding, or an association, between the command "Quiet" and the response of stopping barking, you must first show her what you want.

For one complete month—every time your dog barks—gently grab hold of her collar with your left hand. With your right hand lightly hold her muzzle closed and give the command "Quiet!" You should hold her muzzle gently with your thumb on top and four fingers under the muzzle.

Do not squeeze her muzzle! Squeezing will cause your dog to flip her head back and forth and cry. That's not the response you want. You are just trying to show your dog what "Quiet" means.

Here's a good analogy: Imagine someone asked you in a language that you did not understand to stop talking. If you did not know what they were saying, you would probably ignore their request. However, if every time you spoke, the person gently placed a hand over your mouth and said in that foreign language, "Stop talking," eventually you would understand. The same is true with your dog. You have to *show* her. Remember, you cannot correct a dog with a command you have not taught her.

After one month of consistently showing your dog what to do, you can test her. At this point, if she does not respond the way you taught her, then you can correct her. In order to correct your dog, you will need a water spray bottle. Adjust the nozzle so that it sprays a solid stream. Make sure that there is (*and has only ever been*) just water in the bottle. You *do not* want to spray anything at your dog that could injure her.

When your dog barks, give the "Quiet!" command. If she stops barking, praise her. If she ignores your command, give her an abrupt squirt right in the face and repeat the command "Quiet!" With a few corrections your dog will learn to respond to your command. After a while you may be able to simply say "Quiet!" and show her the spray bottle. Eventually you won't need the spray bottle at all. She will respond immediately to your verbal command.

A squirt of water in the face certainly will not hurt your dog, but it is an affront to her dignity. Most dogs dislike this harmless but effective correction. I've owned Labs who will swim in the sound in February but hate a squirt in the face! But remember, a correction is used *only* after you have *shown* your dog many times what the command means.

If your dog does not interpret a squirt in the face as a correction (some dogs actually like it), you can use a shake can. A shake can is an empty soda can with ten pennies in it. (Be sure to seal the hole at the top of the can with a piece of tape so the pennies do not fly out.) Instead of squirting the dog, shake the can at her after you command "Quiet!" Most dogs really dislike the rattling sound of a shake can.

Unfortunately, "quiet on command" is a useless exercise if your dog barks nonstop while you are away from the house. That's because you must be present to give the command "Quiet!" But what if you have a dog who is "built to bark" and does his noisy barking when you are not home? Here are some things you can try.

First, if possible, pull the shades down or close the curtains or shutters on your windows. Visual stimulation causes many dogs to bark. Some dogs simply see a dog or cat in the yard—or a bird in a tree or a car on the street—and they bark nonstop.

Try leaving a radio or the TV on. The sound may drown out any noises that stimulate barking. I've found that the sound of human voices (even from the radio or TV) can soothe dogs with separation anxiety. These are dogs who bark simply because they are left alone.

Try giving your dog extra exercise. Tired dogs are sometimes too pooped to make a big racket. (This suggestion will sound logical to most dog owners, unless your dog is a terrier. They always seem to have enough energy to bark!)

If you have taught your dog to be quiet on command, you can try the old setup routine. The simplest version of this procedure is to leave the house and wait outside the door. When the dog begins to bark, quickly step back in and give the command "Quiet!" With several repetitions of this setup, some dogs learn to be quiet when left alone.

However, if your dog is wise to this setup, you may have to be more elaborate. You may have to slam your car door and start the motor, then sneak back to the house. A few years back I had one client whose dog did not begin barking until he drove away. This guy had to drive his car down

Terriers can be a noisy lot. Lola, a cairn terrier, does her share of barking, but she has learned that the command "Quiet!" means to stop–at least for a little while.

the street, park it, and sneak up to the door. He would then bust in and command "Quiet!" After two weeks and about a hundred repetitions, his dog finally stopped barking when left alone.

Another alternative is a "bark breaker" training collar, which is a dog collar activated by barking. There are two types: One gives off a high-frequency sound that dogs dislike; the other gives an electric shock. Both are designed to silence a barking dog.

When I was first exposed to this type of collar about twenty years ago, my initial reaction was that I did not like them. It wasn't so much because of the correction that they deliver, but because these collars inhibit dogs from barking. Barking is a normal canine behavior. I believe that it's not mentally healthy for a dog to be afraid to *ever* bark. Of course, excessive barking is another story. It's a nuisance and a disturbance. Your neighbors (and you) should not have to put up with nonstop barking.

I have not personally trained a dog with one of these collars because I've never had a dog with a barking problem. So, unfortunately, I can't give firsthand advice about them. (I'm always most comfortable giving advice on training methods and training tools that I've used myself.) My apprehensions about these collars have been relieved somewhat because everyone I've ever talked to who has used one has told me, "My dog knows when it's on, and he won't bark. But when the collar's off, he's not afraid to bark at all!" The reports seem to indicate that they work well with most dogs. I've yet to hear about any negative psychological backlash from one of these collars.

Despite my wariness about something designed to prevent a dog from barking, they do seem to have a place. If I were going to get kicked out of my apartment, arrested for disturbing the peace, or pressured to get rid of my dog, I would certainly try this type of collar. But try some of the other suggestions first. They are simpler and don't cost a thing.

Gun-Shyness

Dear dog talk: I'm going to get either a black Lab or a Chesapeake Bay retriever to hunt ducks and geese. Should a reputable breeder give a guarantee against gun-shyness?

Dear hunter: No. That's because 99 percent of all gun-shy dogs were made so by their owners. The 1 percent of dogs who come to their owners already gun-shy are usually "everything-shy." They are shy, spooky pups who are afraid of their own shadow. This uncommon type of pup rarely makes a good gun dog.

When you select your puppy, pick one that is confident and outgoing. Then it is up to you to condition the pup to the sound of a shotgun. Here is how I suggest you do that:

Step One

After you have your pup home for a few days and have established a feeding routine, make some noise during mealtime. Clang a metal tablespoon on the inside of your pup's metal food pan as you prepare his three meals. If your pup likes food, he will soon come to associate this noisy racket with his dinner. By doing this, you accomplish step one in forming an agreeable association to a loud sound. Do this with every meal until your puppy is four months old.

Also at this stage you should teach your pup to retrieve. Do this with two tennis balls. Roll one ball down a hallway. When the puppy chases it and picks it up, praise him. Show him the other ball and encourage him back to you. Let him hold the ball in his mouth. Do not be too quick to take it from him. If he drops it near you, praise him. Continue to practice this every day until he is four months old. (Be sure not to overdo the retrieves initially so you don't lose your pup's interest. Toss no more than three or four retrieves per session.)

Step Two

If at four months old your puppy is an enthusiastic tennis ball retriever, you are ready for step two of the "sound conditioning" process. Purchase a pop gun or cap gun. You don't want anything too loud—just something that makes a popping sound. Throw the tennis ball or retrieving dummy. (At this stage you can make the switch to a gun dog retrieving dummy, which is shaped like a big, fat sausage.) As your puppy races out after the dummy, shoot the pop gun. Chances are your pup won't even notice. Perfect.

After you have done this for a dozen or more sessions, your puppy will probably completely ignore the sound of the pop gun. Now shoot the gun *as* you throw the dummy. Don't skip step one: It's important initially that you wait until your pup is racing after the dummy before you shoot. When you first try this step, your pup may look back toward the popping sound and stop retrieving. If so, say nothing and quickly throw another dummy. Encourage him to fetch the dummy. Continue this procedure every day until your puppy is six months old.

Next you need a .22-caliber blank gun or starter's pistol. These can be purchased at most sporting goods stores or gun shops. In many states you do not need a permit to buy a starter's pistol.

Step Three

At this stage of your training, I recommend that you get a friend to assist you. Repeat the retrieving procedure described in the first part of step two using the starter's pistol. After your pup starts to fetch the retrieving dummy, have your friend shoot the pistol while standing about fifty or sixty feet away from you and the pup. Repeat this a dozen times. Do it again the next day, but this time have your friend stand twenty or thirty feet away. With each successful training session, move your friend closer until he is right next to you. When your dog does not react to the starter's pistol at all, then you can shoot it *as* you throw the retrieve, just as you did with the pop gun. Do this every day for six weeks.

Now your seven-and-a-half-month-old puppy is ready to experience the sound of a shotgun. Use the same procedure as described above. Only this time, your assistant should be one hundred yards away (the length of a football field) because of the louder sound that a shotgun makes.

Remember to always introduce a new sound to your pup, whether it's a pop gun, starter's pistol, or shotgun, *as* your pup is chasing the retrieving dummy. Move your assistant toward you slowly. For example, the assistant should spend three days at one hundred yards, three days at eighty, three days at sixty, and so on. Your goal is to have your assistant standing right next to you, but there's no rush. Slow and steady training will produce the best results.

The key to success is letting your dog form an agreeable association to gunfire. *Do not* bring your dog to a turkey shot or when you practice on clay pigeons. Even experienced bird dogs can become unnerved when exposed to incessant blasting of one or more guns. Throughout your dog's life, only expose him to gunfire when he is retrieving or when birds are flushing. People who take a pup into the field and blast a shotgun over their heads without proper introduction are just plain foolish. If they don't ruin their dogs for life, they're quite lucky. Their next dog could easily be traumatized by such treatment and never be able to spend a single day in the field.

Hates the Kennel Crate

DEAR DOG TALK: I have an eight-month-old sheltie mix. He *hates* going into his crate. When we put him in, he growls and tries to bite. Actually, he did bite my eleven-year-old son. The strangest thing is that once he's in the crate, he's fine. It's just putting him in that he hates. What can we do?

DEAR CAGED: First of all, you have to teach your puppy in no uncertain terms that biting is not acceptable behavior. Until you accomplish that, putting the pup into the crate should only be done by adults.

When your puppy growls at you as you crate him, tell him *"Nhaa!"* in a firm, guttural tone. If he turns to bite, grab the loose skin at the scruff of his neck and give a firm shake as you growl "Cut it out!" in a firm tone. Stare directly into his eyes as you do this. Then put him into the crate. As you put him in, tell him "Kennel" or another command word that you choose to mean "Go into your crate."

When your puppy is in the crate, praise him. Open the crate door slowly and tell him "Wait." If he comes barreling out of the crate, growl *"Nhaa!"* and quickly close the crate door on him. Again command "Wait" and open the door, but be ready to close it quickly if he tries charging out. Repeat this procedure until he does not try to run out of the crate. When he hesitates and waits, tell him "Okay!" and encourage him to come out of the crate. Praise him when he comes out on your command.

Then pick him up and put him back into the crate. Repeat the procedure as described above four to six times in a row a few times a day. Before long your dog will learn that when you want him to "kennel," he had better comply. It is very likely that after a few months of practice your dog will get into the kennel on his own in response to your command.

Hates the Kennel Crate, Round Two

DEAR DOG TALK: We have a ten-week-old shepherd/collie mix. I read your book *Dog Talk* and loved it. Your training methods and philosophies make a lot of sense, and we plan to use your book to train our puppy.

I've already started with housebreaking, and Jack (our puppy) has had no accidents in the house since we got him two weeks ago. But he hates his crate! Often when we put him in it he cries, howls, and paws at the door. He's fine in the crate if he is exhausted, and he doesn't carry on at night when we put him in it to go to bed. (The crate is in our bedroom.) But during the day, if we are busy and can't watch him, he throws a fit if we crate him. I feel bad making him do something he doesn't like.

DEAR UNSURE: If I were to give just one bit of training advice about puppies, it would be, Make the puppy do all the things he hates to do! That assumes, of course, that the things you want your puppy to do are for his own good and for the good of your family. As a matter of fact, I also suggest that you eradicate the sentence "He doesn't like it" from your vocabulary when dealing with your dog. Only you and the other adults in your family have the big picture of what your puppy must do to be safe, healthy, well-fed, and properly exercised. Certainly a ten-week-old puppy does not.

Here are some examples from my own household. My black Lab, Byron, hates to have his toenails clipped. If I let him have his way, his nails would grow to all lengths and he would develop serious foot problems. My springer spaniel puppy, Crea, hates having her floppy springer ears cleaned. Too bad! Dirty ears can become infected—and a painful mess. Drifter hates a bath, but he loves to roll in goose poops! So whenever he does, he gets his bath. When my child tells me, "Daddy, I hate brushing my teeth," my response will be the same: "Too bad. You need strong, healthy teeth. Let's go brush them."

Think about the point I am making. How obedient will your dog ever be if he's telling you at ten weeks old, "I'll throw a fit if you crate me"— and then you let him out? That doesn't give a very strong message that you are in charge. I don't think your puppy hates his crate as much as he would rather be out playing with you and your family. That's understandable but not always possible in a busy household. The very worst thing you can do is open the door and let him out when he carries on.

One thing you can do is ignore him and let him learn that his behavior will get him nowhere. Or you can whap on the top of the cage and say, "Cut it out!" in a stern tone of voice. This will let him know in no uncertain terms that you do not like this behavior and will not tolerate it.

If you think I sound unbending and stern, you are only half-right. Rules are rules, and I believe in enforcing them for the good and safety of my dogs and household. But I don't act like a drill sergeant. Pack leaders can be loving and caring while remaining in control. I'll admit that my four dogs are probably the most indulged and spoiled dogs in America! But they are spoiled with love—not spoiled brats.

Aggressive at the Door

D EAR DOG TALK: I have a three-year-old male boxer named Foreman. In the last year Foreman has become extremely aggressive with people who visit our house. When people come to the door he starts barking, lunging, and growling. He is particularly bad with men—he has even tried to bite a few. We tell him "No" but he does not listen. Is there anything we can do?

D EAR READY-TO-THROW-IN-THE-TOWEL: Without meeting you and your dog, it's difficult to accurately evaluate this situation. However, getting Foreman under control would definitely be a good start to solving your problem. It's going to take some work.

The first thing you should teach Foreman is to sit and stay. This means to stay in a sitting position at your left side. He must learn that the command "Stay" means not to move (although he can move his head and wag his tail). He must not move until you release him—regardless of distractions. You can achieve this behavior in about a month if you practice every day. All dogs who go wild at the front door or whenever they meet people should know this exercise. Here's how you do it:

For training equipment you will need a six-foot leather leash and a heavy-gage metal training collar. (Avoid the extra-heavy training collar. It has large links and does not release well.) If Foreman has a high pain tolerance, you will need a pinch collar, which is described in detail in my training book *Dog Talk.*

Begin teaching the sit-stay to your dog in an environment with very little distraction. It is important for the dog to be able to concentrate. Place your dog in a sitting position at your left side. While bent over with your hands on your dog, tell him "Stay." Stand up straight. If your dog gets up when you stand straight, growl *"Nhaa!"* in a firm, guttural tone. Then bend over and replace your dog in a sitting position at your side. Continue to do this until your dog remains sitting at your side for fifteen seconds. After fifteen seconds, tell your dog "Go!" or "Okay!" (or whatever release word you choose) as you simultaneously give a gentle jerk on the collar and take a few steps forward. Praise your dog lavishly.

The next time you practice this exercise, keep your dog staying at your left side for thirty seconds. Each time you practice, increase the designated time that you keep your dog staying by fifteen-second intervals until he stays without moving for three complete minutes.

When you can get your dog to stay at your side for three minutes, you are ready for step two. The goal of step two is to increase the time your dog stays sitting at your side from three minutes to five minutes and also to begin proofing him. "Proofing" means to create distractions that will cause your dog to make a mistake so that you can correct him.

This may sound strange to inexperienced handlers, and often when I suggest this to my students they ask me if proofing is a fair thing to do. They are understandably concerned that they may be teasing their dog. I tell them that it *would* be unfair and teasing if they could simply tell their dog, "Do not move from a stay regardless of what goes on around you." But, unfortunately, that does not work. So you must set your dog up to make a mistake so that you can correct him. Dogs then learn what you want by repeatedly experiencing the consequences of their actions.

The rules of thumb for proofing are simple. Start with mild distractions. When mild distractions do not affect your dog while he stays, introduce moderate distractions. When he remains staying in the presence of moderate distractions, incorporate chaotic distractions.

It's important to understand that every dog is different in response to proofing. What might be a mild distraction to one dog may be a chaotic distraction to another. If your dog gets completely out of control, the distraction is too much. Ideally the distraction should simply cause your dog to move out of position so that you can growl *"Nhaa!"* and replace him.

Some suggestions for proofing distractions include the following:

- Shuffle back and forth around your dog.
- Squat down on his level.
- Clap your hands.
- Bounce a tennis ball (a surefire distraction for golden retrievers!).
- Show doggie treats and drop them on the floor in front of him.
- Have friends and family members walk or run around the room.
- Have a friend say, "Hi, Foreman! How are you doing?" Important: Be sure that no one says, "Foreman, come!" during proofing. This would confuse any come-on-command training you are doing. But your helpers can clap in his face or squeak a toy in his face.
- Get a helper to knock on the door or ring the doorbell. (This may be too much for Foreman at first. Add this particular distraction after you have achieved easier ones.)

If any of these distractions cause Foreman to move from the stay, growl *"Nhaa!"* and replace him in the stay position. With practice, Foreman will get better at containing himself around distractions. That's your goal for step two.

Now it's time to put this exercise to use to help solve your problem.

When you have accomplished the goal of a reliable sit-stay with a variety of distractions, you can begin teaching Foreman to greet people in an acceptable, nonaggressive manner. You teach this by arranging simulated visits with friends and family members. Lots of practice in these simulated situations will help Foreman learn how to behave in actual situations.

Place Foreman in a sit-stay at your left side by the front door. Have a friend come to the door and knock or ring the doorbell. (Remember, knocking or ringing the bell was one of the distractions you practiced earlier.) If Foreman starts to bark, tell him "Quiet." If he moves from the sit-stay position, growl *"Nhaa!"* and simultaneously jerk back on his training collar. Your goal is not to restrain or strangle the dog, but to give him a timely, quick correction for the mistake he made. Replace him in a sitting position and tell him "Stay."

Once Foreman is under control, tell your friend to come into the house. When he enters, greet him: "Hi, Bill. How are you?" Your friend should respond, and then say hello to Foreman. If Foreman tries to break the stay and go after your friend, correct him with a firm jerk on the collar and a tough *"Nhaa!"* Replace him at your side and remind him, "Stay."

If Foreman remains at your side when your friend enters the house, praise him. If Foreman remains calm when your friend greets him, praise him some more. Have your friend offer him a piece of cut-up hot dog. (All dogs love hot dogs!) If Foreman takes the hot dog, praise him lavishly.

Have your friend leave the house, come back three minutes later, and repeat this procedure. In fact, try to repeat this procedure five times in a row. Then try to do this several times a week with as many different people as possible. Your goal is to teach Foreman to remain under control whenever someone comes to the door.

Stay a step ahead of the situation whenever possible. When you see a friend pull into your driveway, clip Foreman on his training collar and leash (which you keep handy *right* by the door). Put him in a sit-stay before your friend even knocks. Each time you do this, you are reinforcing in Foreman the behavior you expect from him. Letting him bark and lunge and bite—because you were not in the mood to deal with him—reinforces an unwanted (and dangerous) behavior.

I know this sounds like a lot of work. It is! But you have a serious problem on your hands. Aggressive dogs are a dangerous liability. The horror stories of bone-crushing bites and mauled children are not fantasies. They are the tragic result of out-of-control animals. So I strongly advise that you deal with Foreman's problem behavior now. If you do nothing, I can almost guarantee that it will get worse.

A few other thoughts on aggression in dogs: I should point out that simply being out of control may not be the entire cause of Foreman's aggression problem. There are many reasons that dogs become aggressive. It could be anything from simply being untrained to medical problems to bad temperament. Also, a dog who thinks he is the household's pack leader will become aggressive. You did not mention in your letter whether or not Foreman is neutered. He should be. Not being neutered can contribute to an aggression problem.

I also strongly suggest that you seek the one-on-one help of a professional trainer who specializes in behavioral problems. This person may be able to determine exactly why your dog is behaving this way and may give you some additional advice more specific to your individual dog. Whatever the outcome, I'd still advise you to teach Foreman how to be under control at the front door. It's a useful obedience exercise that every dog should know.

A Male Who Doesn't Lift His Leg

DEAR DOG TALK: I have a fourteen-month-old husky-shepherd mix that I adopted from the local animal shelter. He is a neutered male and a very good dog. My question is, When will he lift his leg? When he urinates he squats like a girl dog. I really don't care that much but my boyfriend makes fun of him.

DEAR ANXIOUS: Male dogs start to lift their hind leg to urinate when they reach puberty. It's actually a marking behavior to establish territory. The urine scent they leave is sort of a doggie calling-card. Marking lets all the lady dogs in the area know that "super-stud dog" is around and

Mookie, a couch-loving Labrador retriever mix, went many months without lifting his leg like other male dogs. When puberty arrived, he learned this behavior, although not all males do, especially when they are neutered at a young age.

available. It also alerts other male dogs to stay away. However, most male dogs don't run from an area just because they smell another dog's mark; they simply cover the scent with their own mark.

It is sometimes comical to watch these territorial males in action. A roaming male dog will enter another dog's yard (or perceived territory) and leave his mark. The dog who lives there will methodically retrace the steps of the intruder and re-mark all of his territory. This ritual can go on for a period of years! If a roaming male dog is unfortunate enough to get caught on a resident dog's territory, he may get roughed up and run off.

Male dogs who are neutered before they reach puberty often never develop the behavior of leg lifting. Although you may have to listen to your macho boyfriend make fun of your dog, there are many benefits to a male dog who does not lift his leg. One, the dog will never get goofy and feel compelled to mark territory in the house. Two, if you have a nicely landscaped yard, you won't have to deal with a dog burning beautiful bushes and shrubs with acidic urine. Three, taking your dog for a walk on the leash is not interrupted with fifty pit stops at every bush or fire hydrant!

Male dogs who are neutered after they have already started lifting their leg may continue to do it out of habit. Unfortunately, there's not much you can do to make them stop. I have even met a few spayed females who developed this behavior. (I assume that a hormonal influence causes spayed female dogs to lift their leg to mark territory.) The next time you visit your veterinarian, ask about canine leg lifting and marking behavior. I'll bet that with your vet's scientific background, he or she can give you even more information on this interesting subject.

An Owner Who Whimpers at Her Dog

DEAR DOG TALK: I have a nine-month-old miniature poodle. He has been biting me since I got him. I bought a miniature poodle because I thought they were smart and good-natured.

When he bites my hand, I whimper and pretend that he hurt me. Sometimes I don't have to pretend because it does hurt. He always looks like he's sorry, but he does it again and again. Why is he so grouchy? It's enough putting up with my husband who is grouchy. Help!

DEAR HURTING: Miniature poodles *are* very smart and generally good-natured. However, all puppies bite. It is their way of finding where they fit into the hierarchy of their pack. Biting (and being bitten) is an important indicator of who's dominant and who's submissive. If a pack member's response to being bitten is to whimper, then the puppy will continue to bite them, as a sign of dominance. If the pack member's response to being bitten is a tough growl or snap, the puppy will learn to be submissive to that individual.

If a persistent puppy does not respond to the pack member's growl by backing off and acting submissive, a dominant pack member will escalate his or her aggression toward the pup. He may escalate aggression by snapping at the pup. He may grab the pup by the scruff of the neck and give a shake, rolling the puppy belly-up. He may even bite the puppy, causing him to squeal. These techniques will convince even a tough puppy of who the dominant pack member is.

I have found that even the world's most submissive puppy will dominate its human pack members *if* owners do not give the correct signals that they are in charge. This is what seems to be happening in your situation.

In order to convince your poodle that you are *not* a pack member who will tolerate being dominated, you must begin training through a canine point of view. Use "dog talk" to teach your pup that you are the one in charge. In other words, stop whimpering and start growling. *"Nhaa!"* uttered in a deep, guttural tone is the growling sound I recommend.

Consistency and repetition are the keys to success. Dogs rarely learn with one or even a few experiences. You will have to growl many times before your puppy learns to avoid biting you. Remember that pack leaders are consistent. Every time your puppy even looks like he is thinking about biting, growl *"Nhaa!"* Don't tolerate biting from this moment on—not even for a second.

I also strongly recommend that you start your poodle in an obedience training program. You can do this by enrolling in a group training class or hiring a private trainer to come to your home. Obedience training will teach you how to train your dog to be responsive to commands. It will also give you control and enhance your pack leader image to your dog. As I've said to many people before, "If you can't be a pack leader, get an aquarium!" Only pack leaders should have dogs as pets.

Eating Socks

DEAR DOG TALK: I am writing about Cleo, our two-year-old black Lab. She is generally very well-behaved. She doesn't chew shoes or furniture, but she is *crazy* about socks! Thanks to Cleo, my six-year-old daughter has no matching pairs left.

Our concern is that Cleo will do real harm to herself unless this strange habit is corrected. Cleo has no access to socks during the hours when she's alone, and we are monitoring her more closely when we're home. But she's still finding those socks! Cleo sleeps in a crate in our bedroom, and in the wee hours of the morning, we sometimes hear her vomiting, indicating that the socks are not easy to digest. Any bright ideas?

DEAR IN-THE-DARK: Unfortunately, I don't have a magic-wand solution to your problem. Essentially you are already doing the correct thing. Crate Cleo when you are out of the house or cannot supervise her, and monitor her when you are at home.

You also may want to give my rolled-up newspaper technique a try. (Don't pass judgment until you've read the whole description!) Take an old newspaper and roll it up. Wrap some masking tape around the paper to help keep it tightly rolled. Then, whoever leaves their socks where Cleo can steal them gets hit over the head six times as you repeat, "Put your socks away! Put your socks away!" Probably after a few corrections, your family will be trained to put socks away! If Cleo laughs while you do this, praise her and give her a cookie. But never hit Cleo with the newspaper for any reason.

You are correct in being concerned about Cleo's well-being. Some dogs will ingest anything. Although most of the stuff that puppies swallow is passed through or vomited up, some things will get stuck. Socks can become lodged in a dog's intestine and could create an obstruction. Often surgery is required to save the dog's life. Nylon stockings and pantyhose are particularly hazardous.

Along with tightening up the ship by putting all socks away, you can try setting Cleo up. Put her on her leash and training collar. Have your daughter walk by and nonchalantly drop a sock on the ground. As soon as Cleo looks at the sock, growl *"Nhaa!"* and give a jerk and release on the training collar. With lots of repetition, this exercise may discourage her from grabbing socks. You can also try soaking a sock in a product like Bitter Apple or Bitter Lemon (available where pet supplies are sold). The bad taste of a doctored-up sock may discourage her as well.

Techniques such as the two described above work well with some dogs and not at all with others. Some dogs simply learn to avoid socks dropped near them when they are on a leash—but when unsupervised they still chew socks that they find. Some dogs can smell a sock that has been soaked in Bitter Apple from ten feet away but will continue to chew unsoaked socks. However, that rolled-up newspaper technique is foolproof!

Aggressive with Other Dogs

DEAR DOG TALK: I have a three-year-old German shepherd that I got when he was a year and a half old. He had been abused by his previous owner. He is fine with my family but very bad with other dogs. This past spring he attacked my neighbor's twelve-week-old golden retriever puppy for no apparent reason and almost killed her. The attack was completely unprovoked. Since this happened, he has been confined either to our house or to a pen in the backyard. Our veterinarian said that neutering him would stop this behavior. Do you agree? Can he be trained out of this?

DEAR IN TROUBLE: I believe all male dogs who are not used for breeding should be neutered—and neutering certainly cannot hurt your dog's behavior. Whether it will have any effect on this particular problem, I don't know. In fact, no one can know for sure because it's impossible to accurately predict behavior.

My experience and intuition tell me that neutering probably will not make much of a difference in your situation. However, neutered or not, your dog should not have the opportunity to get near anyone's dog again. I *have* found neutering to be very effective with dogs who are aggressive in dominance situations, such as challenging other male dogs who invade their territory. Neutering also helps male dogs who resist training because they want to dominate their owners. Unfortunately, your dog's behavior falls more into the category of predator/prey aggression. This is indicated by the fact that he did not care that the dog he attacked was both a female and a young puppy—and posed no threat to him. He simply wanted to attack something vulnerable.

You asked whether training could teach your dog not to attack puppies (or any other dog). I'm not the correct person to give you a definite answer. My forte in dog training is teaching people to get their young dogs to be obedient. I do not work with dogs who have severe behavioral problems. There are so-called experts in this field, but I'm not a big proponent of "doggie psychiatrists" (dog trainers who are psychiatrist wanna-bes) and their psychobabble. I'm highly skeptical of their success.

As tough as this is to say, I would make the difficult decision—if this were my dog—of putting him to sleep. The world is full of unwanted dogs. The majority of these dogs are sweet, gentle creatures who just need a home. Give this some serious consideration. Also keep in mind that a life exiled to the pen in the backyard is not much of a life.

Nonstop Chewing and Biting

D EAR DOG TALK: I have a thirteen-week-old bulldog named Wilbur. He is doing a lot of chewing and biting. What can I do to stop this?

D EAR BULLISH ON BULLDOGS: Puppies chew on objects such as rugs, chair legs, and shoes because it feels good on their teeth. Unfortunately, untrained puppies don't know the difference between dog toys and valuable objects in your home. In the months ahead, Wilbur's urge to chew may become even stronger. If you allow this behavior to continue, it will develop into a bad habit that could last your dog's entire life. That's certainly not what you want.

You can do several things to prevent a habit of destructive chewing from developing. One is to provide your puppy with appropriate chew toys. I give my puppies nylon bones, rawhide bones, and sterilized natural bones for chewing. I'll describe each briefly.

Some dogs love nylon bones, and some dogs have no interest in them. They are safe and extremely difficult to chew apart. As dogs chew them, the hard nylon develops frizzy surfaces that are supposed to stimulate gums and help keep teeth clean.

Rawhide is a more popular item to many puppies. When I give my puppies rawhide, I always give them large pieces (often in the shape of bones, rings, or large knots). I want to make it difficult for them to chew pieces off. Small chunks of rawhide can be hazardous. These pieces can get stuck in a puppy's throat. When the bone starts to get small or the pup chews a small chunk off, I throw it away. I allow my puppies to have rawhide only when I'm keeping an eye on them.

Sterilized natural bones are generally safe, but many puppies are not interested in them. There is no pungent odor to attract the puppy's interest. However, I discovered a little trick several years ago that works like a charm. Sterilized natural bones are hollow. Place a doggie biscuit or a piece of cheese inside the bone. Puppies will work on these doctored-up bones for hours. I call them "puppy pacifiers"!

"Tired puppies are good puppies" is one of my favorite sayings. It's so true! All the energy that might go into chewing, biting, and other unwanted behaviors can be diffused (at least somewhat) by exercise and play. Linus, a Shetland sheepdog puppy, demonstrates the blissful art of a puppy nap.

Supervising your untrained puppy at all times is also imperative. If you catch your pup about to chew or in the act of chewing something inappropriate, correct him by growling *"Nhaa!"* After you growl, take him away from the item and give him his own chew toy. If you follow these guidelines until your pup is one year old, you will never have a destructive chewing problem.

If your puppy is chewing you (mouthing) or biting, this is a different behavior than chewing on objects. Puppies chew on people to find out where they fit into the hierarchy of the family. If you allow your puppy to mouth or bite you, you are saying to him in his language (dog talk), "You are the boss." If you growl *"Nhaa!"* at him every time he even thinks about putting his mouth on you, he will learn that you are in charge. The key words here are *every time.* Consistency is the key to shaping your pup's behavior. Mother dogs are very consistent and puppies learn at a young age that she is the boss. Your job is to take over where Wilbur's mom left off.

Fence Fighting

DEAR DOG TALK: I own a five-year-old shepherd–golden retriever mix. He was neutered when he was eight months old. He is friendly with people young and old and has never met a dog he doesn't get along with. He is even gentle with cats and bunnies. *But,* when he is in my fenced yard, he turns into "demon dog."

Anyone (outside of my family) who comes near the fence causes him to fly into a vicious rage. My neighbors can't even pull into their driveway without him barking like crazy at them, even though he has seen them come and go for five years. I would think he would be used to them by now!

If their female dalmatian comes up to the fence, he attacks her. He can't bite her because they are separated by the fence, but he bites the fence! The strangest thing is that if my neighbor brings his dog into our yard, they play like they are best friends. The only other time my dog is like this is when we leave him in the car. Is he possessed?

DEAR POSSESSIVE: No, he's not possessed. This behavior comes from his shepherd genes. He is simply being territorial. Your dog has a strong protective instinct, and he feels that it's his job to guard your yard and your car. I'm surprised that he doesn't do the same thing in your house.

Your narrative could have been describing my Australian shepherd, Drifter. He does exactly the same thing (except Drifter hates cats and bunnies!). I have never figured out how to get Drifter to ignore individuals whom he interprets as intruders to his territory. However, I have trained Drifter to stop barking on command and to "cut it out" when I come out into the yard. He is also responsive to these commands when he starts his routine in the car.

When I leave Drifter alone in the car or before I get out to the yard to control him, Drifter always does his protective thing. He thinks it's his job, even though he doesn't get paid for it.

As for your dog "getting used to" your neighbors coming home, the canine brain doesn't work that way. Dogs repeat behaviors that are agreeable to them, and barking at the fence, psychologically, feels rewarding to the protective dog. Canine habits are formed by consistently repeating behaviors. So after doing this behavior for five years, barking at your neighbors when they pull into the driveway or come near the fence is a conditioned response. I doubt that after five years of constant reinforcement this habit can be broken.

I recommend that you start an obedience training program with your dog. Teach him to be quiet on command and to stop whatever he is doing when you command him to. This will not eliminate his protective behavior, but it will give you a way to control him. Also, more "exorcize" always helps reduce demonlike behavior in dogs!

Puppy Stuff

Appropriate Discipline for a Puppy

DEAR DOG TALK: What's the proper way to discipline a puppy? Some friends say to hit him with a newspaper; others say never hit him. Some people tell me to say "NO"; others say this is negative. I'm confused. What do you suggest?

DEAR PUPPY OWNER: I train dogs through a canine point of view. This means I try to communicate the way dogs do. For example, when a mother dog disciplines her puppies, she growls at them. I imitate her. I growl *"Nhaa!"* in a low, guttural tone. Puppies instantly understand what I mean. (This is where I came up with the term "dog talk.") If puppies ignore their mother's growl, she will increase her aggression a bit. She may grab her pup at the back of the neck and give a gentle but firm shake. I do the same thing if a puppy ignores my growl.

Hitting dogs is a bad idea for several reasons. Often it causes a dog to become aggressive. Hitting will also teach your dog to not trust you. Trust is the most important thing that owners can develop with their dogs! Finally, hitting is not a way that dogs naturally communicate. Train your dog through a canine point of view and he'll learn quickly.

Picking the Pick of the Litter

DEAR DOG TALK: A new puppy will be joining our household in a few weeks. The breeder called and said a litter had been born. She offered us the chance to pick out our pup, but we're not sure how to do that. Do you have any advice?

DEAR PUPPY PICKER: By putting some thought and common sense into your puppy selection, you have a much better chance of a long-term, happy relationship with your new pet. It sounds like you have already done some groundwork in finding a breeder that you will get your puppy from. That's great. Your next difficult decision will be which of the cute wiggly puppies you should choose. Not all puppy owners have to make this decision. Many experienced dog breeders choose the pup for you. From years of experience they know which puppy, based on your family makeup and lifestyle, would be best for you.

If the breeder leaves the decision in your hands, you will need a bit of

Chewing on shoes isn't allowed—but sleeping in them is okay! Penny, a Golden retriever, was only three months old when she found this warm (and fragrant?) place for a nap.

guidance. Good health is absolutely the first consideration. Make sure the puppies look healthy and well-nourished when you inspect them. Also be sure to check out the health of the parent dogs. Depending on their breed, they should have hip X rays, eye exams, or other evaluations confirming their physical soundness. Don't brush these things aside. Breeders who charge top dollar for their pups owe you the effort of verifying the health of the dogs they are breeding. Also, don't let claims of "show quality" or "AKC papers" convince you to take an unsound pup. Good health is not guaranteed by the fact that the breeder is involved in dog shows.

The second most important consideration for pet owners is trainability. I have found that puppies who are "middle of the road" in personality and temperament are the easiest to train. Avoid the puppies on the far ends of the social scale. In other words, don't choose the most outgoing puppy or the most reclusive puppy. The most outgoing may be the pup that is always into everything—headfirst! This pup will keep you on your toes twenty-four hours a day.

Reclusive or shy pups lack confidence. They may grow up to be dogs who are afraid of their own shadow. The worst scenario with a shy dog is the "fear biter." A fear biter is a dog who bites when afraid. While it is true that by doing the right things with a shy puppy you can avoid letting him develop into a fear biter, this type of dog is a lot of work. Why go through this challenge if you can avoid it?

I suggest that you choose the puppy who is interested in you without being a complete extrovert. How can you tell? First, evaluate the puppies' reactions when you enter the room. Are any of them shocked or startled by a stranger? Do any of them jump all over you the minute you arrive? Sit on the floor with the litter. A middle-of-the-road puppy will sniff you and check you out. After a short while he may climb into your lap.

When the puppy you are considering climbs into your lap, you can test his dominance level. Gently roll him belly-up with his head against your chest. If he grows and fights violently, he is a dominant pup. Growl "*Nhaa!*" and gently restrain him. If he continues to resist, he is a puppy who has tendancies to lead. He will challenge you at every turn. Only experienced dog trainers will ever succeed with this guy.

If the puppy settles down rather quickly, he is an assertive individual who *is* willing to submit. You will have your work cut out for you, but with good handling and consistency this puppy can be trained. However, he may still be more work than you bargained for.

Another puppy may not growl but will mildly struggle and then stop wiggling and lick you as soon as you say "*Nhaa!*" This puppy will be much easier to train than the two types described above. If the puppy does not struggle at all and just licks you, he is a submissive puppy. He will be easy to train. However, you will have to be careful never to be overcorrective with this gentle soul.

When you have assessed a few of the puppies' personalities, think about your household. Is there a lot of activity and noise from kids and their friends? A puppy who is somewhat outgoing may fit right in. Are you an older person or the parent of a small child? A submissive, easy-to-train individual would be better for you. It's much more common to get a bad *match* between puppy and owner than to actually get a "bad dog." Keep in mind that you're buying a living creature whose best shot at a long and happy life is fitting in well with you and your family.

Sound Shyness

If possible, it's also a good idea to test the puppies for sound shyness. Here's one simple way to do it. Have a friend drop a metal food pan on the floor in an adjoining room (*not* right near the puppies!). You should be sitting on the floor with the pups. Don't say anything to the puppies when the pan drops. Just watch them.

You will see one of three reactions. Some puppies will not react at all. This is good. (If you are evaluating dalmatians, make sure they are not deaf).

Other puppies will look around and go right back to playing. There is no problem with this reaction, either. However, do be careful if you are buying this pup as a hunting dog. You should introduce him to gunfire gradually.

The third possible response is to freak out and run and hide or to shake like a leaf. This puppy will be a dog who is afraid of thunder and will be a gun-shy bird dog. The fourth of July, with fireworks and other noise, is always a nightmare for this poor animal. A car backfiring will scare him. I recommend that you avoid this puppy. In most cases, inherent sound shyness is impossible to cure.

They All Seem the Same!

Sometimes the differences in puppies' personalities are not so dramatic, making your choice more difficult. If it's hard for you to evaluate the puppies, and the breeder or shelter workers are no help, then simply trust your intuition. Do you have a good feeling about a certain pup? Is it physically sound and emotionally stable? Can you visualize it being happy and well-adjusted with your family?

The pup's physical appearance should please you, but personality and temperament are a lot more important. Always be sure to check out the mother and, if possible, the father dog. Puppies usually turn out just like mom and dad. If mom and dad are shy or overly exuberant, extremely aggressive or sound-shy, look for another breeder or puppy source. Problems like these you don't need.

Some dog owners have told me that "the puppy picked us!" That's okay, too, as long as you went into the selection process with a level head. If the puppy's genetic and health background checks out, if the pup's personality seems right, and if the mother and father dog are acceptable, by all means, take home this little bundle. I would never deny that dogs have a sixth sense about people. If the pup picks you, enjoy your good fortune, and make every effort to be the great dog owner your new puppy believes you will be!

The Right Puppy Age to Leave the Litter

DEAR DOG TALK: What is the ideal age for a puppy to be taken from its litter and become integrated into a family? I recently looked at a litter of Westies that were six weeks old. The breeder said she would not let them go until they were twelve weeks old. Is this a problem? One of my neighbors got their shepherd at five weeks old and it's a crazy dog. Could the age they took it have anything to do with its personality?

DEAR PICK-OF-THE-LITTER: To answer your first question, research has shown that the ideal time to switch a puppy from its canine pack into its human pack (family) is between the seventh and eighth week. I got my springer puppy, Crea, on exactly the forty-ninth day. Seven to eight weeks constitutes a strong socialization period, which enhances bonding between puppies and family members.

Many experts believe that the first fear imprint period is between eight and eleven weeks old. During a fear imprint period, any frightening experience has a more lasting effect on the puppy than if the experience occurs at other times in the puppy's life. During this time, you want to be sure that your pup has positive experiences. However, this is an ideal time to begin to teach your puppy that your growl *"Nhaa!"* means to stop whatever he is doing.

I do not recommend getting a puppy at twelve weeks. I know many people do and may not have a problem, but I have seen too many pups taken at this age who are shy and spooky. A lot has to do with how much socialization the breeder has done with the puppies. If the breeder has taken the pups out into the real world to experience sights, sounds, smells, and new people, there may not be a problem. But the puppy who has only seen the environment in which it was born and has only met the breeder's family may fear the world. An interesting phenomenon is that these puppies often show no signs of shyness at the breeder's. It's when you get them home that they begin to act shy.

As far as your neighbor's shepherd goes, being taken from the litter at five weeks old can definitely affect his personality. Puppies learn a lot by interacting with their littermates and their mother during the first forty-nine days of their lives. They learn how and when to be submissive and how and when to be assertive and dominant. They learn this by developing a hierarchy within their puppy pack.

Also in the litter, mother dog teaches the pup discipline. When they nurse too vigorously or chew on mom's legs, she will growl at them. If they ignore her growl, she will nip them. This is "dog talk"! Puppies deprived of this critical learning experience are often difficult to train.

When to Start Training

DEAR DOG TALK: I have a three-month-old Bouvier. When is the proper time to begin training? When I got Sam, the breeder said that I should not start training this breed too early. "Let him be a puppy," she said. A book I have said to wait until the dog is six months old. My veterinarian said to start right away. I'm totally confused!

DEAR CONFUSED: I don't blame you for being confused—you've received a lot of conflicting advice. The ideal time to begin your puppy's *formal* education is at four months old. By formal education I mean training to sit and lie down on command, come reliably when called, and to stay in place. He also could be taught to walk on a leash without pulling and to greet people without jumping on them.

Dogs form habits (good or bad) by consistently repeating behaviors. That's why it is advantageous to start forming good habits as soon as possible. Your dog will achieve his adult personality at two years old. If you start training at four months old, these obedience exercises will be solid, reliable habits by the time he's two.

Starting formal training *before* four months old is often difficult because of the developmental stage that the puppy is in. It would be like starting a four-year-old child in first grade. Some children might be able to do well, but first grade is generally more effective for kids who are six.

Interestingly, canines are capable of learning at three *weeks* old. Most people get their puppies at eight weeks old, so you can certainly start teaching your puppy many things at this age. The training that I suggest with puppies between the ages of eight weeks and four months is what I call "puppy preschool."

Puppy preschool training deals with the very basics, such as housebreaking, which means teaching your puppy to go to the bathroom outside. It also concentrates on stopping mouthing, getting the puppy accustomed to being handled, and introducing the puppy to a leash and collar. During Puppy Preschool, you can get a head start on formal obedience exercises—such as sit, down, stay, and come—by using training techniques specifically designed for young dogs.

Check the publishing date of the training book that suggested waiting until your puppy was six months old before training. You probably will find that your book is at least twenty years old. When I began training dogs in 1972, waiting until six months old was the rule of thumb. Since then, research and progressive training techniques have proved otherwise. Also, dog training originated earlier in this century with military and police dog training. This type of training is too rigorous for young puppies.

I'm not sure what your breeder meant by "Let him be a puppy." Effective puppy training simply encourages good habits while discouraging bad habits (like chewing on rugs and mouthing on people). Playfulness, puppy energy, and adorableness are not taken away! Perhaps your breeder's experience with obedience trainers was with someone who choked dogs, kneed them in the chest, pinched their feet, or enacted other such abuses that dogs sometimes endure in the name of obedience training. That's unfortunate, because puppy training is important. Just as childhood is the proper time to start establishing good behavior in people, puppyhood is the best time to do the same for dogs.

Two Puppies from the Same Litter

DEAR DOG TALK: I want to get two puppies. I figure that they will keep each other company and be happier than one puppy alone. But I've had people tell me that this is not a good idea. Nobody really seems to know why. What are your thoughts on the matter?

DEAR DOUBLE TROUBLE: The drawback to getting two puppies, particularly two from the same litter, is that the puppies will bond closer to each other than they will to the humans in the family. You can somewhat compensate for this by giving each pup individual time and experiences. For example, you can take them on separate walks, car rides, etc. This will help them form a close bond with you and also help build the confidence they need as individuals.

Another drawback is the fact that two puppies means double work. It's hard enough to supervise *one* puppy to avoid housebreaking accidents and chewing mistakes. Two are a real handful. Kennel crates, baby gates, and a lot of energy are minimum requirements for raising two puppies at the same time.

Even if you decide to take on this challenge, you may have trouble getting littermate puppies. It's been my experience that good breeders are unwilling to sell two puppies to a single owner for all the above reasons.

The owner of these three pug brothers—Henry, Cosmo, and Francis—told me that she took my advice to heart about not getting two pups from the same litter—so instead she got three!

Puppy Hassles

DEAR DOG TALK: I have a twelve-week-old Westie that is driving me nuts. Every time I take my eyes off her, she runs into my dining room and urinates. She wants to play constantly, and she bites! Are all puppies this much of a hassle? What can I do to get her to not be such a pain?

DEAR PUPPY PARENT: I don't consider puppy raising a hassle. If I did, I probably wouldn't do it! However, all puppies are a tremendous amount of work. When we get a puppy (or have a child), our lives change. Puppies have certain needs that require our time and energy.

This creates a problem for many people. I've observed that most people are routine-oriented and thrive on predictability. When their daily routine is disrupted by a new puppy, they strive to get back to their old life instead of adapting to the new situation. When this proves to be difficult, if not impossible, then raising the puppy becomes a hassle.

Here's what you need to do. Watch your puppy every second that she is not in her crate. If you see her urinate in the house, correct her with a guttural *"Nhaa!"* and then take her outside. If you are not paying attention to her and she sneaks off and urinates in the dining room, it's your fault. Whatever you were doing that prevented you from watching your puppy is not your first priority anymore! (It was in your old life, but now life has changed. Keeping an eye on your puppy is what's most important.)

"Take two terriers and call me in the morning." Recovering from the flu was a little easier when Molly and CB came for a visit, even if I had to serve as their temporary dog bed.

You do not have to play with your puppy every minute of the day. However, you do have to set time aside a few times a day for play. Daily exercise is important, too. Tired puppies are good puppies.

And keep in mind that puppies only know how to play with you as they would play with another dog. Biting another dog would be acceptable during play, but with you it's not. Discourage her from biting by correcting her with a guttural *"Nhaa!"* every time she does it. *Every time* are the key words here. Also, play games that do not provoke biting. Wrestling is not a good game to play with a feisty little terrier.

When your puppy is four months old, enroll her in a dog-training program. This could be a group class or you can hire a trainer for private lessons. Practice the obedience exercises with your pup every day. This will turn her into a well-trained dog.

If all of this seems like a lot of work, you're right, it is! You have to be prepared to put in the time and do the right things. Otherwise, raising puppies (and kids) will seem more like a hassle than the fun and rewarding experience it can be.

Health and Grooming

Hearing Loss

DEAR DOG TALK: Our thirteen-year-old Yorkie is starting to have hearing problems. Sometimes when we call her or talk to her she can't locate us and sometimes acts frightened. What can we do to reassure her that she's okay? Also, what can we do to make her feel better as her old age sneaks up on her?

DEAR YORKIE OWNER: I have a very special place in my heart for canine senior citizens. A few years back I lost my beloved Jena, a German shorthaired pointer. Jena was a few months shy of fifteen when I had to make the toughest decision a dog owner must face and have her euthanized. One of my current dogs, Byron, a black Labrador, is twelve, and Drifter is now eleven.

Let me start off by clarifying that I'm not a veterinarian. I do suggest that if you have not already done so, set up a consultation with your veterinarian on this subject. Have the vet give your dog a thorough exam so that you're aware of all your Yorkie's old-age health needs. This will give you a guideline as to what you can realistically expect from her. Knowing her limitations will help you determine how to handle her in various situations.

As our dogs become older, they may lose their hearing as your Yorkie has. Their eyesight weakens. They often have hip and leg problems. Arthritis is common in older dogs, particularly the large breeds. Unfortunately, there is not a lot we can do to prevent old-age ailments. One of the hardest things we *can* do is to realize that our dogs cannot do many of the things they once did so easily. One of Byron's favorite activities throughout his life has been a long, hard run in Nantucket's moors and a vigorous swim in the ponds or the sound. Nowadays the walks are shorter and so are the swims. It's my job as a responsible owner to make sure his activities match his changing abilities.

At one time your Yorkie may have been able to be off the leash. She may have come readily when called. Now that her hearing is failing, she won't be able to respond to you as readily. It would be a good idea to keep her on the leash more often. Don't let her get far enough away from you that she panics when she can't see you or hear your call. Be extra careful near busy streets since she won't hear cars or other dangers. If you find that she seems lost around the house, try to keep her in the same room with you. I've found that baby gates in doorways work great for this.

Fortunately for your Yorkie, all dogs rely more on their sense of smell than anything else. The old sniffer—along with the wagging tail—is always the last to go. Touch is important to dogs, too. If she can't hear you say how much you love her, she certainly can still feel it. Gentle strokes and hugs mean a lot to dogs—of any age.

We're very lucky if our canine friends are with us to a ripe old age. Sadly, that ripe old age is only fifteen or sixteen years at most. That's too short! I'm thankful for every day I spend with my dogs. My advice to you is to love your Yorkie and treat her like the queen that she is.

Excessive Panting

DEAR DOG TALK: During this hot weather my dog pants all night long. Is she nervous? She is driving us nuts.

DEAR NUTS: I don't think she is nervous; I think she is just uncomfortable because of the heat. If your dog ordinarily sleeps on a rug or a dog bed, see if she will sleep on the cool tile of the bathroom floor. Make sure there is an open window to provide some ventilation. Dogs do not have pores in their skin the way humans do. They perspire through their tongues and the pads of their feet. This is why dogs pant when they're hot.

Make sure your dog has access to plenty of water. You also can give her a few ice cubes to chew. Wipe her pads, the top of her head, and her belly with a cool, wet washcloth to help her cool down. If all else fails, head to a store and buy her an air conditioner—or you might not get a good night's sleep until the weather changes!

Bathtime Tips

DEAR DOG TALK: How often is too often to give a dog a bath? Are there any special techniques that make the job easier? My new pup seems to hate the tub.

DEAR SUDSY: Bathing a dog more often than every six weeks can be too frequent. Your dog's coat and skin can easily become too dry from frequent baths. However, a dog with oily skin can handle baths more often than a dog with dry skin.

If your oily-skinned dog *does* get a bath more often than every six weeks, use a very gentle dog shampoo. A doggie coat conditioner also can be used on long-haired dogs to help prevent tangles. If you want to keep your dog clean between baths, brushing the dog every day will do the job.

Here are a few things you can do to make bathing the dog relatively fun and easy.

If your puppy (or dog) is small enough and your kitchen sink is large enough, introduce his first bath there. The sink brings your puppy to waist height, which makes it easier on you. Plus, a kitchen is warm and familiar, a good place to start something new.

If the dog is too large for the kitchen sink, use the bathtub. (I never recommend bathing a dog outside with the garden hose. Unless you have a warm-water faucet on your hose, that ice cold water is sure to create bathtime dread!) Be sure to place a rubber mat in the bathtub to prevent slipping, and put lots of old towels on the floor. Wear old clothes or a plastic apron. You *will* get wet.

Use warm water, a gentle canine shampoo (never human shampoo—it's too harsh), and lots of soothing praise—as long as your pup remains calm. Use your tough-sounding growl *("Nhaa!")* to correct unruly behavior. Have a helper keep the puppy in place if you have an especially wiggly or jumpy pup. After a few bathtime experiences, most wiggly pups learn to stand relatively still and accept being washed.

Grooming a long-haired dog like Margaret, a Shetland sheepdog (left), requires a lot more effort than caring for the short coat of a tiny terrier like Molly (right, perched in one of her favorite spots). Ideally, owners should consider grooming requirements *before* getting a dog.

It's important to rinse, rinse, and rinse some more. Soap left in the coat can itch, irritate, and cause dryness. I've found that those hose-with-sprayer attachments for the sink are great rinsing aids. Towel dry your dog with one or more towels to remove as much moisture as possible. Let him finish drying in a warm, draft-free place. This could be his crate in a warm room or a sunny backyard on a summer day.

Some dogs don't mind a little bit of blow-drying with a hand-held blow dryer. My black Lab, Byron, loves the warm air moving around on his coat (but never held too close or in one place too long to burn his skin). My yellow Lab, Bentley, is frightened by the sound of the blower, so trying to blow-dry him just creates a stressful experience. Groomers use dryers, so ideally, it's great to help your puppy learn to tolerate it. As with most everything, start short and easy. You and your dog are not entering a beauty pageant. Clean and dry is all that's necessary.

Keep in mind that your own physical abilities will be a factor in dog bathing—as will the facilities in your home. Certainly a tiny shower stall is no place to wash a Saint Bernard. And a bad back won't make it very easy to lean over the tub to soap up your dachshund. In such cases, you should rely on a well-recommended grooming shop to help you keep your pooch smelling and looking his best.

Life Spans

DEAR DOG TALK: What breed of dog lives the longest? Which breed has the shortest life span?

DEAR RECORD-KEEPER: As a rule, the giant breeds have the shortest life spans, and the small breeds have the longest. Saint Bernards, Great Danes, and Newfoundlands—all considered giant breeds—often live only six years. On the other hand, the average life span of breeds like the toy and miniature poodles, the Jack Russell terrier, and the Chihuahua is fifteen to sixteen years.

Certainly there are exceptions to every rule. I knew an Irish wolfhound, which is the largest breed (sometimes reaching more than 36 inches at the shoulders), who lived to be eleven years old. That was an *old* wolfhound. Yet I have known several small dogs who made it to twenty. A good friend of mine has a cousin who just lost her Cairn terrier at the ripe old age of twenty-two! Medium-sized to large breeds, such as the Labrador retriever and the German shepherd, have an average life span of about twelve to fourteen years.

Neutering and Hunting Skills

DEAR DOG TALK: I have a black Lab. I bought Josh as a hunting dog. Although I am starting to get interested in hunting ducks and geese, I will mainly use him to hunt pheasants. Josh is also a pet. He lives in the house and goes to work with me almost every day. My mom, dad, and sister all think I should have him neutered. Even my girlfriend bugs me about it. I don't have any kind of male hang-up about doing it. I'm just worried that it will affect his ability to hunt. What do you think?

DEAR BIRD HUNTER: Aside from the fact that they're both attached to the dog, there's no connection between your dog's nose and his testicles. In fact, I believe that neutering male dogs makes them *better* bird dogs! For many years I hunted pheasant over a female German short-haired pointer, and there was nothing more annoying in the field than having someone's lunk-headed male dog trying to mount my spayed female. I've seen intact male dogs spend more time lifting their leg on every bush, leaving their mark, than they did hunting for birds.

I have a friend who recently neutered his six-year-old German short-hair because the dog would take off and sometimes not come home for two days. He told me that the neutering helped tremendously with keeping his dog home. He did say, however, that his dog put on weight. But think of the calories his dog must have burned up roaming around for two days straight! Keep in mind that it's not the surgery that makes dogs fat, it's overeating and lack of exercise.

To be in top form for hunting, a good bird dog must get plenty of exercise during the nonhunting season and also be responsive to obedience commands. If your dog fits this description and is "birdy" (meaning that he has a strong instinct to find birds), he should be a great hunting companion. The only thing that may interfere with his hunting drive is his sex drive. So neutering is a logical choice. It also offers some real health benefits, since neutered dogs won't get testicular disease and have a lower risk for infected prostate glands and cancerous anal growths.

"Holding It" Through the Night

DEAR DOG TALK: I have a five-month-old puppy. Dottie is perfect except for one thing. She is completely house trained and never has an accident. At eleven o'clock every evening I take her out for the last time. After she does her business, I play ball with her for about ten minutes. Soon she's exhausted and I put her in her crate for the night, which is in the kitchen.

Dottie has no problem with the crate. She goes in willingly and goes right to sleep. But every night at three A.M. she wakes up and starts crying and howling. If I go down to her immediately and take her outside, she will eliminate. If I don't get to her quickly, she'll urinate in the crate. Even when I do get her out in time I can't go back to sleep because she barks and cries and wants to play! When will she be able to hold it all night? My husband is really getting fed up.

D EAR SLEEPY: I think your puppy is capable of holding it through the night now. What seems to be happening is that when Dottie wakes up in the middle of the night and sees that her pack (you and your family) is missing, she feels abandoned. When this happens, she begins crying and howling in frustration. After working herself into a frenzy, she loses control of her bladder. Then when you finally show up, she does not want you to leave her again. So she decides that if she can stimulate you to play, you will stick around.

It is natural for canine pack members to "den" together. I suggest that each evening you move Dottie's crate into your bedroom and place it right next to your bed. (If moving the crate back and forth between the bedroom and the kitchen is a hassle, purchase or borrow another crate that you can keep upstairs.) Chances are very good that if you let your puppy sleep in the room with you, your problem will be solved. The puppy will wake up in the middle of the night, see or smell that you are there, and then go back to sleep.

If your puppy wakes up and does start to whine or howl, bang a few times on the top of the crate with your hand or a book (preferably a copy of *Dog Talk* or *Puppy Preschool!*) and tell her in a firm tone, "Quiet." The startling effect of the bang on the crate will stop her crying. At the same time, you will be associating the command "Quiet" with her behavior. Eventually you will not need to hit the top of the crate. Just the command "Quiet" will get her to clam up.

It might take a week of banging on the top of the crate and saying "Quiet" before you finally make it through the night, but your efforts will be worth it in the long run. Your dog's behavior soon will be under control and your marriage will be saved. Plus, you'll be teaching your dog a very useful exercise, quiet-on-command, which can be put to use at any time of day or night.

Keep in mind that dogs form habits up repeating behaviors. At five months old, your puppy has not been on earth long enough to have any deep-seated habits. However, if you let this nighttime behavior repeat itself too much longer, you *will* allow a bad habit to form. So start working on this problem right away. You don't want to spend the next ten to fifteen years getting up at three A.M. to let your dog out.

The many people I have counseled over the years with this problem have told me that as soon as they moved their puppy into their bedroom, the problem went away. It never fails.

One final thought: Never rule out the possibility of a medical cause for a problem such as this. An undetected bladder infection or other ailment could be the cause of trouble. However, Dottie's excellent bladder control during the daytime doesn't suggest it. If my suggestions don't help, your next stop should be the vet's.

One-Eyed and Wonderful

DEAR DOG TALK: My sister's veterinarian has an eight-week-old puppy at his clinic that is up for adoption. My sister would like to adopt him but is somewhat hesitant because the puppy has a missing eye. He was injured when he was a few weeks old and the eye had to be removed. I was told by someone who met you that you have a dog with one eye. Do you feel that this is a severe handicap for a dog? Will it make training more difficult?

DEAR SISTER: I do not believe that having one eye makes life too difficult or unpleasant for a dog. That's because vision is not the sense that dogs rely on the most. Smell and hearing are the dog's primary senses. It's amazing what they can do with those senses alone. In fact, I've met old dogs who have gone blind without their owners even being aware of it! The dogs could navigate just fine around their own house and yard but then would have difficulty at the veterinarian's office. The vet would discover the blindness during an examination.

My black Lab, Byron, who is twelve, lost his left eye when he was seven. He has done remarkably well. He still hikes and swims just like before. He finds his way around any new environment without any trouble. The only change I can think of is that he doesn't catch popcorn from his left side as well as he used to! Encourage your sister to adopt that pup. If Byron is any indication, one-eyed dogs have especially loving hearts.

This is Byron, my one-eyed black Labrador retriever, with his friend Julie. Byron is as gentle and sweet as any dog I've ever known. He manages just fine with one eye—the nose, ears, and wagging tail still work perfectly!

Flea Wars

DEAR DOG TALK: Help! My dog has fleas and is itching like crazy. The spray I use hasn't really worked. Do you have any tricks for getting rid of them?

DEAR FLEA-SPRAYED: I wish a simple trick or two would do the job, but fleas can be a complicated problem. Understand that treating the dog is not the only thing you should be doing. The dog's environment must be made flea-free as well.

Start with a trip to the veterinarian to get medical advice for your dog's condition and professional-strength flea products to deal with the fleas. A flea bath or a flea "dip" (actually a liquid that is sponged or poured on the dog) will probably be your first step. Do this only as frequently as recommended—some chemicals are too strong to use every day or even every week.

A flea comb, which has very fine teeth, can be used on your dog several times a day. As you stroke the comb through the dog's hair, it picks up live fleas. Crush the fleas in your fingers or dip the comb in a cup filled with hot water and soapy flea shampoo.

Your vet my suggest that your dog wear a flea collar. I've found the collars to be more effective on small dogs than large dogs. A large dog's neck is awfully far from its hind end, which is where fleas especially like to hide.

Vacuum your house every day, and put a cut-up flea collar into the vacuum bag. This helps kill fleas that are sucked into the bag instead of allowing them to crawl back out onto your floor. Wash your dog's bed frequently to kill eggs that are waiting to hatch and hop onto your dog.

Flea bombs, or foggers, are products that spray each room with an insecticide. They will kill fleas that you can't vacuum up or wash away. The chemicals in them are strong, so be sure to follow the manufacturer's directions carefully. A professional exterminator can also treat your home with insecticides.

I've had success with the pill form of flea control, called Program, which is available from veterinarians. It works by interrupting the reproductive cycle of the fleas, not by killing them outright. A single pill is given to the dog once a month, year round. The chemical (which is harmless to mammals) circulates in the dog's body and then is absorbed by any fleas that bite your dog. The eggs that these fleas lay cannot hatch. This approach does not work overnight, so use other plans of attack to deal with an immediate flea problem. However, Program seems to be an effective tool for long-term defense against these annoying insects.

Also, try to minimize your dog's contact with other animals who may have fleas. This means dogs and especially cats. Unfortunately, cats are not bothered by fleas as much as dogs are, but they are great flea carriers. If you own a cat, try to keep the cat flea-free. It will help your dog's problem.

Some dogs are allergic to flea bites (actually to the flea's saliva), so even after you get rid of fleas, you may have an itchy dog. Your vet can help you identify this problem and prescribe medications to control the itching and allow your dog's skin to heal.

Autumn is an especially tough time of year for dealing with fleas. A dog's warm body is an inviting place when the weather turns cold. Whenever possible, stay ahead of a flea problem. One or two fleas will quickly become dozens unless you take immediate preventive steps.

Snipping Ears and Puppy Dog Tails

D EAR DOG TALK: I would like to buy a Doberman pinscher puppy. The problem is that I don't believe in cropping ears and docking tails. Do you know a breeder who does not practice this cruel mutilation? Why do breeders do this to dogs and do you agree that it is cruel?

D EAR UNCROPPED: I don't know any Doberman pinscher breeders personally. I recommend that you ask your veterinarian if they have any clients who breed Dobies. Also check the advertisements for breeders in the back of *Dog World* and *Dog Fancy* magazines. If you meet someone with a Dobie that you like, ask the owner where they got their dog.

After you obtain the names of Dobie breeders, you will have to screen each of them to see if they crop ears and dock tails. If they do, ask if they can make an exception for you and leave your puppy au naturel. If the breeder's purpose for breeding Dobermans is to exhibit dogs in American Kennel Club dog shows, chances are good that they crop and dock. One of these breeders may be willing to sell you a pet quality puppy with a long tail and floppy ears.

For the most part, breeders crop ears and dock tails for purely aesthetic reasons. With Dobermans, cropped ears give them a meaner, tougher look. A Dobie with floppy ears looks like a sweet hound dog! Breeds such as the pit bull terrier, used for the barbaric sport of dog fighting, have their ears cropped so that their canine opponents cannot grab hold of an ear during a fight.

While I agree with you that ear cropping is cruel, I do not have a problem with tail docking. The reason I feel this way is because tails are docked when puppies are three days old. At this age the bone in the tail is thin and soft. Snip, snip with a pair of surgical scissors and the job is done. (I have assisted many veterinarians with this simple procedure.) Also, at this point in their lives, canines are incapable of learned behavior, so this quick procedure appears to have no lasting negative effects.

On the other hand, ears are cropped when the puppy is between eight and twelve weeks old. Puppies are fully capable of learned behavior at this

Doberman pinschers often sport docked tails and cropped ears. Princess has natural ears, which gives her a sweeter look–to match her personality.

age, and as a result I believe that ear cropping is very stressful to them. Puppies have to be put under a general anesthetic, and when they wake up they have extremely sore, tender ears. There is also a lot of postsurgical care that most puppies hate. I can't see putting any dog through this just to obtain a certain look.

Nail Clipping Without a Struggle

DEAR DOG TALK: I have a seven-month-old German shepherd–golden retriever mix. Sandy is a good puppy in every way, except she hates having her toenails clipped. One time I cut a nail too close and made it bleed. Now if I touch her feet she gets nervous. Any suggestions?

Dear nail clipper: Yes, I have several suggestions. First you must gain Sandy's confidence when you handle her feet. Four times a day you should sit on the floor with Sandy and gently handle her feet. Take each paw and gently touch each toe. When Sandy accepts this, praise her in a soothing tone. If she enjoys doggie treats, give a small tidbit after you finish handling each foot.

If Sandy struggles and pulls away when you touch her feet, tell her "*Nhaa!*" in a low, guttural tone. Do the same thing if she growls or tries to mouth your hand. Then continue to handle her feet. If she gets *really* nasty and tries to bite, you will not be able to do the nail-clipping on your own. I would then suggest you get the help of a professional trainer or groomer.

If you are successful handling her feet, repeat this procedure four times a day for two weeks. Separately from handling Sandy's feet, work on this other procedure. Have Sandy sit, show her the toenail clippers and give her a doggie treat while you praise her. After two weeks you can gently rub each foot with the toenail clipper. Praise her as you do this. After each foot, give her a treat. Repeat this procedure four times a day for two weeks. If you are successful with this procedure you can now try clipping her nails.

The key to successfully clipping a dog's toenails is to try *not* to do a good job. That is, just nick the tips of each nail. If you clip back too far, you will hit the "quick" (a blood vessel) and cause the nail to bleed. Some dogs have white toenails so you easily can see the pink blood vessel. Dogs with black toenails make toenail clipping a little more difficult.

Although your dog will not bleed to death, cutting into the quick will hurt her. If it hurts, your dog is not going to want you to clip her nails again. If you do accidentally make your dog's toenail bleed, apply pressure with a paper towel for a few minutes to stop the bleeding. There is also a product called Quick Stop that works well. But try very hard to avoid cutting back too far.

As a dog's toenail grows, so does the blood vessel. When you clip the toenail, the blood vessel recedes back. So each time you clip the tip of the nail, you move the quick back slightly. Frequent nail clippings are the answer for shorter nails. One extreme nail-chopping session is definitely *not* the way to achieve that.

Until my dogs are about a year old and are used to having their nails clipped, I have someone (usually my wife and writing partner, Barbara

McKinney) assist me. Barbara places the puppy in a sitting position on her left side and kneels down next to him. She slides her right hand through the puppy's collar. She reaches her left arm around the puppy's back and uses her left hand to lift the puppy's left leg. The best place to lift the front leg is from the elbow, because it prevents the puppy from pulling his left leg back. Barbara praises him calmly if he does not struggle. She tells him *"Nhaa!"* if he does struggle to get him back under control. Then I clip his nails.

To clip the toenails on the back feet, we have the puppy lie down on his side. Sitting on the floor, Barbara holds him gently from behind and slightly lifts each hind leg while I clip the nails. After the procedure is complete we both praise lavishly and the puppy gets a treat. Although our dogs are not thrilled about getting their nails done, they accept it without a fight.

If my description of this procedure still does not inspire you with confidence, ask your veterinarian or dog groomer to show you how to do it. Although your vet or groomer will do it for you when they see your dog, toenails may need to be done about every two weeks. It's an easy job that all dog owners should learn how to do.

When Your Dog Loses a Friend

DEAR DOG TALK: I have two dogs. Marty is a fourteen-year-old male German shepherd mix. Suzie is six years old and is part Collie. My problem is that Marty is not doing real well. He has arthritis in his hips, and his kidneys are failing. We know that it is just a matter of time until we have to make a decision about putting him to sleep

All of this brings back memories of putting another dog to sleep when Marty was a puppy. It was so sad to see how much Marty missed her. I would not have believed a dog could be affected that way. He improved some when we got Suzie as a puppy a year later, but he never was his old self. My question is, what can we do differently to help Suzie when Marty's time comes? She is like his shadow and really loves him.

DEAR LOVING OWNER: Of all of the questions I've been asked over the years, this may be the toughest one. Dealing with losing our pets is truly the hardest part of dog ownership. I've experienced it myself and wish there was a way to avoid the deep sadness and grief that accompany a pet's death. But for those of us who love our animals, there's no getting around it.

First off, let me state that I'm not a pet loss counselor. Some family therapists offer grief counseling, and there are professionals who provide specific counseling to help people deal with pet loss. A psychotherapist friend of mine offers this service in Connecticut. She's a devoted animal-lover, owns animals herself, and is caring and understanding of the pain associated with pet loss. You may want to explore this avenue further.

The best I can do to answer your question is to share with you my knowledge of dogs and to describe some recommendations I've read and heard about.

Keep in mind that dogs are pack, or family-oriented, animals. They are dependent on the social interaction of the pack, and each family member is important within the group. I don't know whether our dogs view us as other dogs or whether they think of themselves as humans. However, I definitely believe that dogs think they are the same thing we are. As a re-

"Labs in Love." Bentley (left) and PJ (right), both yellow Labrador retrievers, live in different households but have been pals for most of their lives. Like people, dogs do bond with each other and feel loss when a dog friend dies.

sult, we and the dogs in our household become the pack. Like humans, dogs develop relationships with their family members. And, like humans, dogs are often devastated when a family member is lost.

Adding a new member to the pack can certainly give the grieving family members something to focus their love and energy on. This new member will never replace the other. But instead of dwelling on our loss, we become distracted—and fulfilled—by the joys of the new individual. This new members helps fill a void.

Unfortunately, there is no formula to follow to get over pet loss. You may or may not be ready or able to get a new dog immediately. When you are, a new dog often helps ease the pain.

One of the most interesting suggestions I've heard about helping dogs deal with losing a pack member is to let the dog see and sniff the deceased dog right after it has been put to sleep. The veterinarian that suggested this technique felt that it would help the dog understand what became of its pack member. She felt that if we did not do this, the dog would only understand that its pack member was missing, with no idea of what happened to him. This makes sense to me. Barb and I have decided that we will try this technique with our dogs when the unfortunate day comes when we lose a pack member. I hope that day is a long way away. My thoughts are sincerely with you and your pack as you deal with losing Marty.

A Healthy Feeding Schedule

DEAR DOG TALK: I own a three-month-old black Lab. I feed her three times a day. Her first meal is at seven A.M., lunch is at one A.M., and dinner is at six P.M. She seems to have about a dozen bowel movements a day! At what age can I begin feeding her once a day?

DEAR POOPER SCOOPER: That's a lot of dog waste to be cleaning up. I hope you have a big yard! You can cut her back to two meals a day when she's between four and five months old. However, I suggest that you always feed her twice a day. Many large breeds, including Labs, are prone to a condition called gastric dilatation. The more familiar term for this condition is bloat. Veterinary researchers have found a lower incidence of bloat when large dogs are fed two smaller meals several hours apart as opposed to one large meal.

It is also advisable not to feed your dog immediately after strenuous exercise or to exercise your dog immediately after eating. About a one-hour leeway period is a good rule of thumb. Ask your veterinarian about gastric dilatation for a more accurate description of this condition. He or she may also have more tips on how to avoid this problem.

Also ask your veterinarian about the food you are feeding your puppy. A dozen bowel movements a day seems like a lot, even for a puppy eating three times a day. Many of the supermarket dog foods have high bulk and seem to go right through puppies. You may find that a premium food would cause your dog to eliminate less and ultimately be more nutritious.

The Largest Litter

DEAR **DOG** **TALK**: This is not a training question, but hopefully you can answer it. Do you know how many puppies were in the largest litter in the world?

DEAR **RECORD-KEEPER**: According to the book *Dog Trivia,* written by Judy and John Doherty and published in 1986, two different dogs hold this record. One is a Foxhound, the other a Saint Bernard—each produced twenty-three puppies in a single litter! I once assisted an Irish wolfhound in delivering seventeen puppies!

Calculating Dog Years

DEAR DOG TALK: Is the formula "seven human years to every one dog year" accurate? I have a female beagle who will be sixteen in September. Will she really be 112 years old?

DEAR AGED: To be honest, I really don't know. In fact, I have no idea how scientists figure out these formulas! However, an aging formula that I once read about in a dog magazine seems to make more sense to me than the one you mention. The system works this way: At two years, a dog reaches adulthood. This is comparable to a twenty-one-year-old human.

Byron, my black Labrador retriever, and I are the same age in this picture—calculating in dog years, that is. However, we're still arguing over which one of us is the coolest.

Then add four human years to every one dog year after that. This formula would make your Beagle only seventy-seven years young!

On Eating Poop

DEAR DOG TALK: I hope you will respond to my letter—this is not a joke. I have a three-year-old puli who eats poop! (I also have three small children, so I'll try to use adult language. He eats feces.) None of my friends have ever heard of a dog doing this. Is this normal? Can my kids get sick from the dog? Is there any way to stop this disgusting behavior? I can tell when he does it, because his breath stinks and sometimes he throws it up in the house. I apologize for this gross letter, but I'm tired of this problem and I'm desperate!

DEAR POOPED-OUT: This is a great question to ask your veterinarian. I'll do the best I can to share with you my experience with poop-eating dogs. I owned one: Jena, the German shorthaired pointer. She loved all kinds of poop. (For the record, I don't need "adult language." Around my house, feces are called poopies!)

To answer your question, I don't know if this behavior would be considered normal or abnormal. Humans are conditioned from the time they are children that poop is dirty and disgusting. Dogs don't understand our concept of the word "disgusting." (Actually, my Australian shepherd, Drifter, thinks a warm soapy bath is disgusting!) To a dog, poop is probably just reprocessed food.

I would definitely advise you that you get medical information from both your veterinarian and pediatrician on whether or not your kids can get sick. It may be possible that intestinal parasites, such as hookworm or whipworm, could be transmitted to the children if they handled or ingested feces. (This could possibly happen if the dog carried feces into the house or vomited his "snacks" indoors.) I certainly wouldn't let the kids kiss the dog on the lips! I also wouldn't let the dog lick my face. Even if I couldn't get worms, I'd want to avoid her breath!

As for training her not to eat poop, here is what I did with Jena. Initially, I followed her around the backyard, watching her closely. As soon as she headed for the first pile, I bellowed, *"Nhaa!"* in a guttural tone, as I firmly shook her by the loose skin at the back of her neck. After three corrections, Jena never went near poop again—if I was standing nearby. However, if I wasn't around she attacked it like it was a baked ham in the Amazon River!

I knew that if I wanted to keep Jena away from poops all the time, I would have to do something to make poop-eating unpleasant when I was not around. One of my dog training books suggested pouring Tabasco sauce on the poop. When the dog gets a taste of hot, spicy, tangy poop, his poop-eating days will be over.

So every day for two weeks I seasoned every poop in the yard. It worked like a charm. After I finished my third gallon of Tabasco, I tested Jena. Without missing a beat she started grazing. Jena could tell a Cajun poop from six feet away! Finally I gave up. I could not think of a way to modify Jena's poop-eating behavior without investing in stock in a pepper sauce company.

I decided to alter the environment instead. I bought a pooper scooper, and every day I picked up poop. This did not cure Jena's behavior, but it greatly minimized her poop-eating opportunities.

Jena lived to be fifteen years old and occasionally ate a poop here and there. But keeping the yard clean and watching her closely on walks—so that I could get in a well-timed *"Nhaa!"*—limited her hobby. I hope these suggestions help, and if any of my readers have any proven cures, please let me know.

I hate to memorialize Jena as nothing but a poop eater. Outside of this gross habit, she was a great girl and one heck of a bird dog.

Side Note

I got a lot of response to last week's "poopie" column. One reader called to tell me that there is a product on the market called Forbid. If you mix Forbid into your dog's food, it will make his poopies taste bad. (Can you imagine that poopies ever taste good?) As a result, the dog will learn to avoid eating them. However, it will not stop the dog from eating other animals' poopies.

I also found the following information in the book *Dog Owner's Home Veterinary Handbook,* published by Howell Book House. (Every dog owner should own a copy of this book.)

Eating Stool: Coprophagia is the name given to the habit of eating stools—either the dog's own or another animal's. Some stools have a taste appeal to dogs, particularly those containing partially digested foods. Once established, the habit is difficult to break.

Do not allow your dog to eat stools—both for aesthetic reasons and because stools are a source of intestinal upset and carry germs and parasites.

Treatment: A poor quality diet may be at fault. Feed high quality dry kibble as a base with canned meat supplement not in excess of 25 percent. Sprinkle a meat tenderizer (such as Adolph's) on the food as an aid in its digestion. A product called Forbid (which is made from alfalfa) works well when added to the diet. When digested, it gives the stool a disagreeable odor and taste.

That's the poop. Hope you've had a good summer. Welcome, fall!

Overcoming Car Sickness

DEAR DOG TALK: I have a five-month-old American Eskimo dog who gets car sick. After five or ten minutes in the car he begins to drool, and if I don't pull over and let him out immediately, he vomits. Is there anything I can do?

DEAR SICK OF CAR SICKNESS: Like some small children, some puppies are prone to motion sickness. Also like most children, puppies usually outgrow this problem. In the meantime, there are some techniques you can try to help your puppy overcome this unpleasant behavior.

First, make sure your puppy has eaten his previous meal at least three hours before getting into the car. Take up his water at least one and a half hours before the car ride. (Of course, this works only if you can plan your pup's car trips ahead of time.) Also, be sure that your puppy has the opportunity to go to the bathroom a couple of times in the hour before getting into the car. Following these guidelines should reduce your pup's queasiness and will at least help minimize the mess if your pup does get sick.

You may already do this, but be sure that your pup travels on an old towel or mat in the car that can be easily washed. Keep a roll of paper towels in the car, too. An easy cleanup will keep *your* stress level down as you deal with this problem.

You may be able to desensitize your puppy to motion sickness with a gradual increase in his time spent in the car. At first, simply put the pup in the car on the passenger seat next to you while you sit in the driveway with the car's motor running. Do this every day for ten days.

Next, drive up and down the driveway several times, no more than two or three minutes per session. After ten days of this, drive around the block once or twice. Give your puppy ten-day intervals to adjust, continuing to increase the car rides by a short distance.

In time you may see great results. Over the years I've had clients tell me that this system has helped tremendously. Others have told me that *nothing* helped until their puppies finally outgrew the problem. The good news is that of all the dogs I've met over the years, very few adult dogs are bothered by motion sickness.

A final thought: If you are scheduled to take a long trip with your puppy in the near future, you may not have time to try the procedures I've described. Your veterinarian may be able to prescribe a drug that will minimize or eliminate your dog's car sickness. Unfortunately, these drugs are impractical for short car trips because they often "zonk the puppy out." Constant drugging of an animal certainly is not the solution, but drugs may help during occasional longer trips. Discuss your motion-sickness situation with your veterinarian. He or she may have some additional helpful suggestions.

Alexandra, an English shepherd, and Riley, a collie, both love car rides. A comfortable place to travel can help minimize stress and carsickness in vulnerable dogs.

Obedience

What Are Spike Collars?

DEAR DOG TALK: I've had dogs my entire life and trained them for several years with a local dog training club. The trainers I worked with never allowed spiked collars to be used. I can't believe how many dogs I see nowadays with this type of collar. Do you know why?

DEAR OBSERVANT: I'm going to assume that the collars you are seeing are not spike collars. Spike collars have sharpened points that stick into the dog's neck when the collar is pulled tight. This type of collar has been outlawed in the United States for several decades. What you're probably seeing are pinch collars, or what are sometimes referred to as prong collars.

A pinch collar does not stick into the dog's neck in any way. It has prongs that are flat on the ends. These prongs pinch the dog's neck when pressure is applied to the collar. I have never seen a pinch collar leave a red mark, cut, or bruise on a dog's neck. It's a type of training tool that is appropriate only for dogs with a very high pain tolerance.

A pinch collar is one of three different types of collars I use when I train dogs. One type is a flat, nylon or leather buckle collar. Each year, about 5 percent of the dogs I work with are extremely pain sensitive. A buckle collar works well for training these dogs.

About 90 percent of the dogs I deal with have a moderate pain sensitivity. I train these dogs with a metal training collar, or what is sometimes mistakenly referred to as a choke collar. This name is a misnomer because the collar chokes the dog only when it is used improperly. For example, if you allow the dog to drag you down the street or you purposely constrict the collar around the dog's neck, it will choke him. Dogs learn nothing when they are being choked except to be frightened of the person choking them! This collar is used correctly only when the handler jerks and immediately releases. The correction is then applied across the back of the dog's neck, which is a strong, muscular part of his body.

The other 5 percent of dogs that I work with are extremely pain *in*-sensitive. These stoic individuals have necks of steel! They are appropriate candidates for a pinch collar.

Despite its medieval appearance, the pinch collar is not as potentially dangerous as a training collar. A training collar used improperly could act like a noose and choke a dog to death. Pinch collars do not constrict around the dog's throat. They simply pinch. But a pinch is an overcorrection for 95 percent of dogs. It should be used only on the appropriate dog.

A pinch collar can be the difference between success and failure when training a stoic dog. I remember several years ago a gentleman who was enrolled in one of my group training classes with his black Labrador retriever. The dog was a year old and weighed about 85 pounds. After the first class I told him that I doubted that he would ever successfully train his dog with a training collar. I suggested a pinch collar. He said, "What's a pinch collar?" When I showed him, he said, "I'm not putting that on my dog."

I said, "No problem. Good luck."

On the third class he said to me, "I've been working with this dog every day and cannot control him on the leash. Last night he dragged my wife on her belly across the front yard. Let's try the pinch collar."

I put the collar on the dog, and he did well in class. I sent the collar home with the dog and told the owner to call me if he had any questions. I didn't hear from him at all that week. The next week he walked into class with his dog walking calmly on a loose leash. The dog wasn't pulling or gagging like before. I asked him, "How's your pinch collar working?"

"Power steering!" he replied.

On the right dog, the pinch collar is a great training tool. However, I recommend that an experienced trainer make the decision to use one on a dog. A pinch collar is the *wrong* collar for aggressive dogs, and it's not a substitute for bad handling skills. Trainers who are closed-minded to the pinch collar or simply have no experience using it are unnecessarily dooming 5 percent of their students to failure every year.

Teaching a Dog to Come

DEAR DOG TALK: I've owned dogs my entire life and have never had one that came when called. I now have a ten-week-old sheltie pup and would like very much to successfully train her to come. Can you help me?

DEAR SHELTIE OWNER: Yes! Coming on command seems to be the biggest problem pet owners have with their dogs. However, it's the training exercise that dogs in my courses learn the quickest and enjoy the most. I've spent a lot of time working to understand why dogs do—and do not—come when called. Here's some useful advice.

Dogs fall into three distinct categories with coming. Category One is the dog who *never* comes when called. This dog typically has little or no relationship with his owner. He spends his life locked in a pen or tied to a tree in the backyard. When the chain breaks or someone leaves the gate open, this dog is gone. He'll see you at dinnertime or maybe the next day. When you call him, he's not even going to look at you!

Category Two is the dog who will come when he feels like it. This dog usually has a good relationship with his owners. He lives in the house. His owners play with him and take him for walks and for rides in the car. When this dog is loose, he'll come running when called—*if* there is nothing more interesting going on. If there is a bush to sniff, or the neighbor's cat is in the yard, or there is a kid to follow down the street, forget it. You might as well be calling to a brick wall. This dog, who is typical of most family pets, has probably never been trained to come or mistakes were made with the training.

Category Three is the dog who comes reliably when called. This dog is trained to respond immediately to your command. He has what is called a conditioned response to the command "Come!" This dog is a joy to own. He can go for walks on the beach, runs in the moors, and even be free in your backyard while you work in the garden or have a cookout. Your voice is all that's needed to keep him under control.

(Keep in mind, however, that learned behavior is never infallible. This is true with both humans and canines. Dogs can make mistakes. Use common sense when and where you take your dog's leash off. Even with a well-trained dog, you should never take the leash off near a busy road.)

To turn your new puppy into a Category Three dog, there are several things you must do. First, you must show your dog that coming to you is absolutely the greatest thing he could ever do. You want him to think that if he doesn't come when you call, he's missing something! Whenever he comes to you, praise him enthusiastically. Pet him, kiss him, and give him a treat. *Always* make coming to you a wonderful experience.

This means, of course, that you should never call your puppy to correct him. Doing so would undermine your goal of making coming to you wonderful. For example, if your puppy picks up something that's not his, the time to correct is just as he is picking it up. Once the object is in his mouth, it's too late to correct him. Instead, call your puppy to you and then praise him for coming. Gently take the item from him and give him one of his own toys. If you have to go to the puppy to get your item back, do not go chasing after him. This usually starts the annoying game of "you-can't-catch-me." Instead, calmly walk to your puppy, praise him, and trade your item for one of his toys.

It is important that whenever you call your puppy, you must be aware of your body language and your verbal tone. Do not tower over your puppy shouting, "Come, or I'll kill you!" in a harsh tone. When you do this, your threatening body language and verbal tone triggers your dog's flight instinct. When the flight instinct is triggered, dogs run away. That's the exact opposite of the response you want! Instead, squat down on your pup's level, which will make you look more inviting. Use an exuberant, happy voice to call your pup. Clap your hands and make lots of pleasant, happy noise to keep his attention. Most dogs, especially puppies, find this irresistible and will run to you. Now *that's* the response you want.

Also, have an object of attraction in your hand to help your dog come running when you call. The object could be a tennis ball, a squeaky toy, or a biscuit. Showing your puppy something that he likes—as you squat down and call him in a high-pitched, happy tone—often tips the scales and gets the puppy running to you. Keep in mind that every time you call your puppy and he does come running, you're one step closer to forming a solid habit. That's because dogs learn by repeating behaviors consistently.

If all of this fails and your puppy just looks at you, try this: Stand up and run in the opposite direction away from the dog. This will trigger the dog's chase reflex. All dogs have a reflex to chase things that move quickly. (This is what makes cats such doggone fun for dogs.) The motion will cause your pup to come running after you. When he starts running, wave the object of attraction toward him, squat down on his level, and praise him as he comes to you. When he reaches you, praise the daylights out of him! Make him think this is the greatest thing he has ever done in his dog life.

What Not to Do

There's a great way to undo all your conditioning efforts. It's what I call "practicing not coming." Practicing not coming means taking your dog off the leash and standing there shouting "Come! Come! Come!" while your dog ignores you. In dog training, practicing means the same thing as repeating. By repeatedly shouting "Come!" while your dog ignores you, day after day, you're practicing not coming! Instead, keep the leash on your dog in situations where you know from experience that your dog will not come. If you are using the word "Come" and getting the opposite response, you are practicing *not* coming on command.

Getting a dog to come reliably involves one more important thing: using training techniques that are designed to *teach* your dog to come. (Despite what many owners hope for, dogs do not figure this out on their own!) Good training is essential if you want good results. On-leash exercises for come-on-command are outlined with photos in my training book, *Dog Talk.*

Perfecting Come-on-Command

DEAR DOG TALK: I have a problem with my dog. Tuck does not come when called. He and I attended one of your group obedience courses at the Community School last year. The course was wonderful, and he responds to all of the other commands. But if he is distracted he will not come. I think I know what you are going to say: "Continue to practice the come-on-command exercises that you taught us." But he does them perfectly on the leash! It's off the leash with distractions that we have a problem.

DEAR STUDENT: You are right. I encourage you to continue to practice the on-leash come-on-command training techniques that I taught you in class. Let me explain why.

"Mookie, come!" This big, energetic Labrador retriever mix goes on lots of dog hikes because he comes reliably when called. *Every* dog can be taught to do this well.

Eventually you reach a point in obedience training where you can reinforce most of the obedience exercises in everyday living by simply using them. For example, every time I walk my ten-month-old springer puppy, Crea, on the leash, I employ the controlled walking technique. Whenever I cross streets or greet people on the street, I make her sit and stay. Every night when we eat supper, she does a down-stay. At night when I flea comb her, she has to stand and stay. So all of these behaviors get reinforced on a daily basis simply by being incorporated into everyday life.

Come-on-command is a bit different. It's the one exercise for which I have to set aside ten minutes every day and practice in a formal manner. If I do not, the best I can hope for is a dog who comes when she feels like it. Remember that every time you take your dog off the leash and call him—and he does not come—you are actually practicing "ignore the command 'Come.'" If you do this, you are teaching your dog that he does not have to come when called.

Dogs form habits by repeating behaviors consistently. Every time you do one of the on-leash training techniques, you are one step closer to forming a conditioned response to the command "Come."

As you learned in class, the key to making the transition from on-leash work to a successful off-leash response is keeping the leash loose at all times. The only time the leash should ever tighten is when you are giving a correction with a quick jerk and release on the training collar. Dogs who are trained by being guided on a tight leash become leash dependent. They may respond well on-leash but either have no clue what to do or learn that they do not have to respond when the leash is off.

As part of your daily on-leash practice, you should also increase the distractions in your training environment. From your dog's point of view, there's a big difference between on-leash work in a quiet setting and running free with lots of people and dogs to divert his attention. Build up his ability to pay attention to you in a busier setting. For example, try some on-leash practicing along one of the bike paths or somewhere in town. Does Tuck often ignore you during your hikes along the beach? Do lots of practicing in that environment.

Practice come-on-command every day for one year. If you do this, I promise that you will have a dog who responds reliably to the command "Come!" Also, do not take the leash off in situations where you know from experience that Tuck does not come when called. This will only undo your hard work.

Coming Even When Your Dog Doesn't Want to

DEAR DOG TALK: I'm working really hard to train my golden retriever to come when I call him (none of my other dogs ever did). He's doing okay with the training exercises, but he completely ignores me when we go for hikes. He would rather sniff bushes, greet people, play with other dogs, etc. How can I teach him to come in these situations?

DEAR GOLDEN TRAINER: Your situation is made-to-order for a simple but very important training tool: the long line. A long line is simply a thirty- or forty-foot length of rope (such as clothesline or thin boat rope) with a dog clip attached at one end. They can be purchased ready-made, or you can make your own with supplies from a hardware store. Unlike the dog's training leash, you do not hold the long line. The dog drags it behind him.

During hikes on the beach or along nature trails, the long line gives you the upper hand. When an untrained dog (or partially trained dog, like yours) is free and unclipped from a leash, *he* has the upper hand. And the wide world is usually a very enticing place. If your dog does not feel like coming when called, all you can do is stand there practicing not coming by indiscriminately calling "Come! Come! Come!" with no response. That will eventually undo all your hard work of teaching your dog to come when called.

When your dog is clipped to a long line, you call your dog once. If he does not respond, don't even worry about what the dog is doing. Look for the end of the long line. Step on it before you pick it up, and run in the opposite direction. (Never grab a moving rope. You will probably get a painful rope burn.) Running in the opposite direction will trigger chase reflex and cause your dog to come running after you. If he does not come running, he will get a tug on his collar, forcing him to come.

Use your object of attraction to induce the dog directly to you. (This prevents him from running past you.) Be sure not to reel him in like a bluefish on the end of a fishing line. Coming *always* has to be agreeable. Praise your dog as he is running toward you. When he reaches you, make him think it is the best thing he has ever done! Give him lots of praise and hugs.

The long line enables you to keep the dog coming to you until a solid habit of coming reliably is formed—no matter what's going on around him. If your dog has already learned that the sound "Come!" means to run in the opposite direction, you may want to choose a brand new word that means "Run to me now!" Be sure that it's a short word and easy to shout out. Your command may need to be heard across a big field or on a noisy beach. "Puppy, please come here" just won't do!

A few safety tips for using a long line: The long line should *only* be attached to the dog's buckle collar. Never use it with a training collar or a pinch collar. Be careful that the line does not get stuck around a bush or tree. Also, watch that the line does not wrap around anyone's ankles—your own or people nearby. A person could easily be knocked down if this happens with the line attached to a large dog (especially in winter if the ground is slippery with ice or snow). Even a line attached to a small dog could result in a nasty rope burn. Small children should not be present when exercising your dog with a long line. Although the long line is a very effective training tool, it should always be used with caution.

Using a Kennel Crate Safely

DEAR DOG TALK: Is using a cage to train a dog a good idea or is it cruel?

DEAR CONCERNED: Used correctly, a cage (usually called a kennel crate) is a very effective training tool for housebreaking a puppy or older dog. It's also effective for providing a structured environment during the first year of a dog's life. The crate helps prevent unwanted destructive chewing, which can quickly become a bad habit if the dog is free to chew on things when left alone.

Crates can be misused, however. Never leave a puppy in a crate during the daytime for more than four hours at a time. Puppies cannot control their elimination needs longer than that. Long confinement to the crate forces puppies to eliminate in the crate, and this is counterproductive to your housebreaking goal. At night puppy metabolisms slow down and puppies can control their bathroom needs for up to eight hours.

Never use a crate to punish a dog. Exiling the dog to the crate after it misbehaved will teach the dog nothing. In fact, social deprivation is cruel.

Finding a Qualified Obedience Instructor

DEAR DOG TALK: I have placed a deposit on a golden retriever puppy that we will get next month. When Nellie's old enough I plan to do obedience training with her. My neighbor had a horrible experience with a dog trainer, so I'm a little nervous about finding someone good. Any advice?

DEAR **NERVOUS** **NELLIE:** I've found that there are a lot of *un*-qualified people claiming to be obedience instructors. It's important that you be selective. Here are some insights into what to look for in a trainer.

Actually, I'll start off by telling you what to avoid. Avoid any instructor who advocates so-called training techniques that involve kneeing dogs in the chest, hitting dogs, or stepping on or pinching their toes. These procedures are abusive and unnecessary. I tell people that if they find themselves in a training class where that's happening, *walk out.* No dog should be subjected to such abuse. Period.

Also, avoid instructors who feel it is their role to humiliate, badger, or intimidate you into working with your dog. That kind of treatment never motivates people. An obedience instructor's role is to set up a training program for you, teach you humane training techniques that work, and try to inspire you in a positive manner to practice with your dog each day.

If a group training class is the format you are interested in, be sure to observe an instructor's class prior to enrolling. Evaluate the class. Are you comfortable with the instructor's demeanor? Do you like the way he or she interacts with both the human and canine students? Do the training techniques appear to be something you will be comfortable doing with your dog? Listen to what the instructor is saying. Does it make sense?

When screening an instructor on the phone, ask the right questions. How long have you been involved with obedience training? How long have you been teaching people how to train their dogs? Do you have a dog? Answers to these questions will give you some idea of the trainer's level of experience.

Of course, longevity does not mean qualified. In most states, training dogs and teaching people how to train their dog is *not* a licensed profession. It's not even state-certified. Anyone can print up business cards or place an add in the paper calling themselves a dog trainer. That's why it's up to you to call around and screen each trainer you call.

Don't be afraid to ask for references. It's understandable if instructors are reluctant to give out their clients' personal phone numbers. However, they should be able to provide you with the names of veterinarians, groomers, and pet-supply store owners who have received feedback about the trainer. These professionals can tell you if their clients have been satis-fied—or not.

The trainer's demeanor on the telephone is also something to consider. Are they explicit with what they have to offer? Does their training course sound wishy-washy and unstructured? You don't need an obedience instructor to help you train haphazardly—you can do that on your own! You want a trainer who offers an organized, step-by-step program. Is the trainer willing to answer questions over the telephone? A trainer should not have to come to your home and charge you for a visit when they could easily handle a small problem in a short time over the phone.

Find out if the trainer is a professional. It's impossible for someone to teach you something that they do not know. I've found that trainers who earn their living training dogs have experience that hobby trainers do not.

Finally, keep in mind that your dog is a family member with whom you will be living for twelve years or more. The investment you make in training during that first year will pay off for many years to come. Sadly, some people spend more time and energy shopping for clothes or household appliances than they do for a good dog trainer! I'll never understand that. It's always worth investing the extra time and expense to work with a qualified trainer. Good luck and good training with your new puppy!

Jumping on People

DEAR DOG TALK: I have a German shepherd who is fourteen months old. He's a very good dog but he loves people *so* much that he jumps all over them. A training book I bought suggests kneeing him in the chest. I'm afraid to do this because I don't want to hurt him. Is there any other method that will work?

DEAR JUMPED-ON: Do not knee your dog in the chest. That's a lousy method. More often than not it doesn't work, and you're right—you *can* injure your dog. I've seen X rays of two different dogs who were severely hurt by owners attempting to knee them to prevent jumping.

Understanding your dog's motivation for jumping will help you solve your problem. Dogs greet people by jumping on them for one reason: They want attention and acknowledgment. First, train your dog to stay reliably in a sitting position for up to five minutes. Practice with the leash in your hand and the dog directly at your side. When you have achieved this goal, practice this sit-stay exercise around distractions, such as TV sounds, a bouncing ball, even a knock at the door.

When your dog can sit and stay during five minutes of distractions, you are ready to use the sit-stay during a greeting. Tell your dog to sit and stay (be sure you're holding his leash) and then have a visitor approach. If the dog breaks the stay when the person attempts to pet your dog, have the greeter *back away.* Correct your dog both verbally and with a gentle, quick tug back on the leash. Re-sit the dog and have the greeter approach again. Only when the dog remains in a sitting position will he receive what he wants: attention! Before long your dog will understand that if he sits when he greets a person, he will be petted. This technique takes daily practice, but it works well, is not cruel, and won't hurt your dog in any way.

Early Learning Abilities

DEAR DOG TALK: I'm getting a Lab puppy in a few weeks and am really excited. I know that training is important, but when do I start? Someone told me to wait until she is six months old, but I've met some six-month-old pups who are really bratty. Is it okay to start sooner? I don't want to be too harsh, but I don't want an obnoxious dog, either.

DEAR PUPPY PRESCHOOLER: Teaching your pup good habits should start the very day you bring her home—when she's about seven weeks old. She can start to learn her name, where to go to the bathroom outside, to stop mouthing you, how to wear a buckle collar, and so on. These are the types of exercises in my puppy preschool program, which is for pups up to four months of age. Then they are old enough to begin formal obedience training.

In fact, canine behaviorists have determined that the optimum learning period in a canine's life is between the ages of seven and twenty weeks old. EEGs (electroencephalograms) of seven-week-old puppies have been shown to be identical to those of two-year-old dogs. This means that by the time your seven-week-old puppy arrives in your home, its brain is fully developed and the pup has its full capacity for learning. All that is lacking is experience, which the puppy gains on a daily basis.

If your dog were a wild canine, such as a wolf or coyote, during this phase in her life she would start following adult pack members into the woods to learn behaviors essential to her survival. For example, she would learn to avoid porcupines and poisonous snakes and to trail rabbits. It is *instinctive* to follow direction at this point in a young canine's life.

The same is true of your domestic dog. She is going to learn during this period regardless of whether you supervise what she learns or whether she learns haphazardly on her own.

Unfortunately, some trainers, breeders, and veterinarians still recommend waiting until a dog is six months old to begin obedience training. By the time puppies reach this age, the instinctive, optimum learning period has passed, and canines enter a phase in which they begin to assert their independence. In the wild, wolves and coyotes begin wandering off with littermates to explore their environment without adult supervision.

Owners of domestic dogs often find that their six-month-old puppy—"who *never* has left the yard"—is now down the street at the neighbor's. Puppies at this age become less and less dependent on the security and safety of the den (your home) and on the guidance of adult pack members (you and your family).

In addition, by allowing six or more months to pass before obedience training begins, owners run the risk of letting unwanted behaviors, such as chewing furniture and jumping on people, develop into bad habits. Those are probably some of the bratty young dogs you have met.

By the time a canine is eighteen months to two years old, she will have achieved her full adult personality. It is at this point in your dog's life that, if she has done whatever she pleased, whenever she pleased, she may have assumed the role of boss (pack leader). If this has happened, your dog may interpret attempts to obedience train her as a direct challenge to her assumed pack leadership role. She may resist this challenge in much the same manner an old wolf would resist being ousted by a subordinate in the pack—by growling, biting, snapping, etc.

This is what can make training an older dog difficult, if not impossible. However! The cliché "You can't teach an old dog new tricks" is a fallacy—unless your dog has reached a stage where she is completely resistant to learning and resists in a violent manner. Clearly, it's to the owner's advantage to start obedience training early.

That's why I recommend Puppy Preschool training right from the start, followed by formal training at four months. Neither of my programs is harsh or run with a "drill sergeant" attitude. Training should be a positive experience both for you and the dog. And that time spent training at the beginning of your dog's life will have lasting benefits for the next twelve and fifteen years. It's one of the best investments I know of.

A Harness Instead of a Leash

DEAR DOG TALK: I have a Siberian husky who thinks I'm a sled! He drags me down the street even though he is choking half to death. I have used a choke collar but that makes him gag and cough even worse. Are you familiar with a Halti? I use this and it works great, but people are constantly making comments. Some people have even said it's mean to use.

DEAR SLEDDING: Yes, I'm familiar with the Halti, a modified horse's halter designed for dogs. Haltis are not mean to use. They do not hurt a dog in any way, and they *do* restrain dogs from pulling. I don't use them, however, because I believe in training dogs, and the Halti does not teach the dog anything. It simply restrains the dog, and I've found that restraint will never teach a dog anything. In other words, you can use a Halti for ten years and, while it's on, the dog will not pull. But any time your dog's not wearing the Halti, he will drag you down the street.

Training a dog to walk on a leash *without* pulling requires either a buckle collar, a training collar (sometimes called choke collar), or a pinch collar. The proper technique is to prevent the leash from ever becoming tight. The handler must give a jerk-and-release correction before the leash becomes tight. With practice and good handling, you can teach the dog not to pull—and he'll be under control for the rest of his life!

From the description in your letter, it sounds as if you were not using the training collar properly. Or perhaps your dog was the proper candidate for a pinch collar. I'm glad that you at least stopped the routine of dragging you on a leash. Continuous pressure on your dog's throat with any type of collar can create a chronic cough. If for some reason you are unable or unwilling to train your dog not to pull on the leash, I would prefer to see you use the Halti than to have your dog pulling and choking when you walk him.

Private Versus Group Training Classes

DEAR DOG TALK: I read that you offer an in-home, private training course. How does that work? Do you think it's better than group classes?

DEAR TRAINEE: I'm asked this question frequently. My private in-home training course consists of five lessons that are designed to teach owners how to train their dogs. It's a structured course. I meet with my client once every two weeks. Each of the lessons is approximately two hours long. I say "approximately" because the lessons are not based on time. I don't look at my watch and say, "Whoops! Your time is up; I have to run." Instead, I have a specific lesson plan for each lesson, and we work until I've completed my agenda and all of my client's questions are answered.

I've found that dogs learn the fastest and owners have the most success when training exercises are broken down into simple steps. A step-by-step approach is the basis for all my training. On the first meeting I show my student step one of several different obedience exercises. The owner then practices step one with their dog every day for two weeks. Then, on lesson two, I show them step two of each exercise. We continue in this fashion through all five lessons. By the fifth lesson the dog should be doing what I call the "end result," or finished version, of each exercise. Then it is up to the owner to continue to repeat the exercises until they become deep-seated habits.

The exercises I teach in this course are sit and down-on-command, plus stay from a sitting, standing, and lying down position. The course also includes come-on-command, controlled walking, and heeling. My courses are not obedience-competition oriented; they are pet-oriented. This means that I do not put an emphasis on precision and the tricks you would do only in the ring at an obedience trial. Instead, we cover other

This isn't a group obedience class—just six dog friends doing a sit-stay together on the beach. Obedience training allows dogs to enjoy a lot of freedom and fun in their lives.

useful behaviors such as greeting people without jumping, quiet-on-command, stopping mouthing, achieving housebreaking, and avoiding destructive chewing.

During each two-hour lesson, I also teach dog owners some canine behavior. This helps owners understand how dogs think and learn. I explain to my students the purpose of each exercise and how the training technique is performed. Then I demonstrate the technique with the dog, showing the owner how it's done. Then I have the owner perform the technique with the dog until both dog and owner are doing the exercise correctly.

At the end of each lesson I give the owner a detailed reference sheet that reiterates each exercise in detail. Also included are relevant articles about canine behavior. In fact, everything we do throughout the lesson is written down for the owner to look back on.

The people who do well with my courses make training their dog a priority. They keep each of our appointments and try to work with their dog every day. That's a lot of work! One of my favorite sayings is that if it were easy, everybody would have well-trained dogs—but unfortunately, most people do not. But my approach to training makes the course work fun. I don't teach like a military boot-camp instructor. I also don't use abusive training techniques, such as kneeing the dogs in the chest, choking them with training collars, or pinching their toes. The dogs themselves provide me with the best feedback—they love school!

My private lesson course is better than a group class for several reasons. With private lessons I get to see where the dog lives and how he behaves in his own home. I can teach owners a lot more about training their specific dog (and about dog training in general) when I'm talking one-on-one to a family as opposed to when I'm talking to a group of people about a group of dogs. Owners find practice is easier to accomplish if they have two weeks to work with their dog—as opposed to the one week between group classes. Also, private lessons can be scheduled more flexibly. If the owner does not feel well, goes away on vacation, or simply needs more time to practice, they do not lose a lesson. Group classes meet once a week whether you show up or not.

Certainly the expense of private lessons is greater than for a group class. My clients pay for the course in full on the first lesson, and I do not give refunds to dropouts. Although my fee structure for private obedience instruction is close to top of the line in the United States, my course is top of the line! I really believe in my program because for more than twenty-five years I've seen it produce satisfied owners and happy, well-trained dogs.

All About Obedience Trials

D EAR DOG TALK: I have a Shetland sheepdog that was born last year. She is a very good puppy. I have been obedience training her using your *Dog Talk* book and she's doing well.

You have pointed out in your book that the type of training you do is pet-oriented and is not designed for obedience competition. I *am* interested in participating in obedience trials and have several questions. (I noticed that the bio in your book said that you earned many obedience titles.)

These are my questions: Will training my dog using the exercises in your book inhibit my dog from being successful in competition? What book or books do you recommend that are competition-oriented? How do I find out where competitive obedience events are held? What exactly does one have to do to earn an obedience title? And last, I'm curious to know why you no longer participate in this type of training.

DEAR COMPETITOR: Wow! You may keep me in front of the keyboard for a month answering all of your questions. But that's my job, so I'll do the best I can. Let me start by saying that the obedience exercises I teach in my *Dog Talk* book are designed to help owners control their dogs. These exercises are very similar to the exercises used in the first level of obedience competition, which is called "novice." The difference is that the major focus in obedience competition is on precision. I put no emphasis on precision when I train dogs to be well-behaved pets. My emphasis in training is on achieving a quick and animated response. Although speed and enthusiasm also are assets to the competition dog, precision is the major factor by which you and your dog will be judged.

I really don't have a specific book that I recommend for competition training, although there are many available. I do recommend that you subscribe to *Off-Lead,* a dog trainer's magazine. Trainers often submit articles on competitive obedience training. *Off-Lead* also reviews training books, many of which you can buy directly through the magazine. The mailing address is *Off-Lead,* 204 Lewis Street, Canastota, NY 13032. The phone/fax number is (315) 697–2749.

There's a second publication called *Front and Finish,* which is even more competition-oriented, although I personally don't find it as interesting. The mailing address is P.O. Box 333, Galesburg, IL 61402.

Off-Lead and *Front and Finish* magazines both are good sources for locating upcoming obedience trials. There's also a publication called *The Match-Show Bulletin,* which is dedicated to informing its readers about upcoming obedience events. I do not have an address for this publication, but as soon as you start to get involved with the world of dog showing, all of this material seems to fall into your lap.

I'm glad to tell you the criteria for earning obedience titles with your dog and to share with you why I no longer compete in obedience trials.

Let me preface my answers by saying that some of the rules may have changed since I last competed in 1980. To acquire up-to-date rules, write to the American Kennel Club, Inc., 51 Madison Ave., New York, NY 10010.

Only purebred dogs who are registered with the American Kennel Club are eligible to complete in AKC obedience trials. Three basic obedience titles are available: Novice, Open, and Utility. When your dog has earned a title, certain symbols of achievement appear after his name on his AKC pedigree: CD for Novice, CDX for Open, and UD for Utility.

In order to win a title, a handler and dog must earn three qualifying scores, under three different judges, at three different obedience trials. A perfect score in a trial is 200 points. Ribbons, trophies, and sometimes cash are won by the top four dogs and handlers closest to a perfect score.

A qualifying score is 170 points or better. To earn a qualifying score, you cannot receive fewer than 50 percent of the points assigned to each exercise. In other words, if your dog fails an entire exercise, you will not receive a qualifying score no matter how well you do with all the other exercises.

To compete in the Novice class, your dog must heel on-leash in a pattern specified by the judge and in a figure-eight, stand for examination, heel off-leash, recall (come on command), sit-stay, and down-stay.

In the Open class, the exercises are off-leash heeling, drop on recall (lie down on command while coming), retrieve on flat and over a high jump, a broad jump, a three-minute out-of-sight sit-stay, and a five-minute out-of-sight down-stay. Dogs must have earned a CD title to compete in the Open class.

Utility exercises include scent discrimination of small objects, a routine directed by hand signals only, directed retrieves, a heeling pattern ending with a stand for examination, and directed jumping. A CDX is required for dogs to compete at the Utility level.

In the final years that I competed in obedience trials, the American Kennel Club created the title "Obedience Trial Champion," or OTCH. This title can be earned only by dogs holding a Utility title. To achieve an OTCH, the dog and handler continue to compete in Open and Utility classes in order to accumulate points toward the title. (Based on how many competitors participate, each trial is assigned a certain number of points.) One hundred points earn the dog an OTCH title.

There are many reasons why I no longer train dogs for obedience competition. Mainly, I became burned out and bored. I earned fourteen titles on nine different dogs in about six years. I was on the road more than half of each of those years, every Friday through Sunday, criscrossing the eastern half of the United States from Washington, D.C., to Maine.

Also, I became disenchanted by the competitive attitudes of many of the handlers. To many of them, winning was everything, even if it meant exploiting their dogs to do so. I became progressively uncomfortable with some of the training techniques that were being advocated and also with the obvious stress that continuous drilling brought to the dogs.

Only in the Novice class do the obedience exercises somewhat parallel obedience that is useful in everyday life. The two advanced classes, Open and Utility, involve exercises that, to me, are nothing more than "stupid pet tricks." Roll over and play dead are as useful to most dogs as any of the exercises in Open and Utility!

All of the top trainers I met were experts at obedience-trial procedures and the techniques required to teach their dogs obedience-trial exercises. To my dismay, I found that some of these "experts" had very little true understanding of dogs. I saw many dogs with obedience titles who were perfect in the show ring but could not even come on command at the beach. Keep in mind that a dog can be extremely well trained and obedient without ever going within fifty miles of a dog show!

I have mixed emotions about my past experience with obedience competition. Some of the experiences certainly helped me with my career as a professional dog trainer and obedience instructor. But I now think that my talents as a trainer would be squandered if I redundantly put my efforts

"Aaah, a cool dip in my pool with my stuffed banana toy." Monty, a Golden retriever, shows how puppies in Florida like to have fun. If you have a pool, make sure your dog is *always* supervised when in or around it.

into teaching dogs to do "tricks." Dogs mean too much to me for that! The majority of dogs who get put to sleep each year do so because their owners don't know how to train them and make them behave. Teaching these owners and working with these dogs are where my passions lie.

I'm sure an individual with the proper perspective and a good attitude can have fun with obedience competition—without placing too much pressure on their dog. Just keep in mind that it's the handler who receives the ribbons and the accolades in the winner's circle. The dog couldn't care less. So no matter how much he appears to enjoy competing, he would enjoy a hike in the woods ten times as much.

An Experience with an Abusive Trainer

DEAR DOG TALK: Something happened with my eight-month-old golden retriever, Amber, that I really would like your opinion about. My fiancé and I hired a dog trainer to come to our house and help us train Amber. This trainer came highly recommended by one of the local pet boutiques and by a veterinarian. We love our dog and were looking forward to training her, but the experience we had was disappointing and upsetting, to say the least.

When the trainer arrived at our house, we introduced ourselves and Amber. The trainer abruptly stated that she was not going to greet Amber just yet; first she was going to talk to us. Of course, Amber was very excited to have a new person in her house and was jumping and wagging her tail enthusiastically. The trainer talked to us for a while, telling us different things about dog training and our dog. Some of it seemed to make sense and some did not.

One of the things that seemed most odd was the suggestion that we should ignore Amber for a half-hour when we first get home from work. The trainer told us that dogs are not equal to humans and that this technique would teach Amber that we are superior to her and that she would think of us as pack leader. But Amber is *so* friendly and outgoing, I think she would completely lose her mind if we did not say hello to her! Besides, my fiancé said that we didn't get a dog to ignore her, we got a dog to be a family member. I feel that way, too.

This story gets worse. By the time the trainer finally got around to interacting with Amber, our friendly dog was reluctant to come near her. I don't know why—other than she picked up on the trainer's demeanor and it made her nervous and afraid. Maybe she sensed that my fiancé and I were uncomfortable. Nevertheless, when Amber balked at coming at her, the trainer grabbed the leash and dragged her toward her over a stool (which then toppled over).

Needless to say, Amber, my fiancé, and I were all very upset at this point. We tried to not overreact or let our emotions get out of hand. We got through the rest of the lesson but have no intentions of ever having this person near our dog again. I'm now reluctant to get involved with any training because, like I said, this person came with good references. I'd really like to know your thoughts and feelings on this incident.

Bentley, the champion! Actually, he's sporting an "Honorable Mention" medal for participating in a Frisbee contest. Having fun was our goal, and for that he would have won the grand prize.

DEAR VICTIM: I'm very sorry that you, your fiancé, and especially Amber had this type of experience with obedience training. Although stories like this always dismay me, I can't say that they shock me. I hear *dozens* of similar tales every year from dog owners throughout the United States. Unfortunately, there are a lot more *lousy* dog trainers and obedience instructors offering their services than there are good ones. Really great ones are a rarity.

I'm compelled to first addressed the "big picture" behind your specific situation: the fact that there is no standardization of dog training methods or training philosophies. In most states, dog training is not a licensed profession. Dog trainers are not state certified. *Anyone* can print up business cards and call themselves a trainer.

As a result, dog training classes can be taught by ineffective or even abusive trainers. Many trainers have a confused understanding of dogs, and as a result, they have convoluted training philosophies, leading them to give out idiotic advice and to suggest ridiculous training techniques. I wish I could say that I'm exaggerating to make a point, but I'm not. The stories I constantly hear make me want to scream.

The fact that you got good references makes the situation even more complex. Unfortunately, most pet boutique owners and even many veterinarians are not experienced with quality obedience training or even know how to evaluate the field. But because they are inundated with requests from their clients for a recommended trainer, they often refer individuals who "seem like nice people." As you painfully discovered, seeming like a nice person does not make someone a qualified obedience instructor. Your intuition was right: You were dealing with an incompetent trainer.

I'd like to comment on the "training technique" that the trainer recommended to you, which was supposed to establish your pack leader status with the dog. (The technique was to ignore the dog for the first half-hour after the owners came home.)

Anyone who has studied canine behavior is aware that domestic dogs, like their cousins the wolves, have a greeting ritual that is an integral part of their social order. Whenever an individual enters the den area, he or she is greeted by the pack. During the greeting, each pack member gives signs, such as body stance, indicating that member's rank in the hierarchy of the pack. Although body language may differ slightly from one individual to the next, no pack member—*particularly* the pack leader—ignores the new arrival.

If you do ignore your dog for the first half-hour after you come home, you would be giving the dog a confused signal. Initially, this technique would make the dog so wound up and frenzied that by the time you finally greeted her, she would be completely out of control. That's not the kind of behavior you want to encourage.

After repeating this scenario for a number of days or weeks, your dog would probably next interpret your behavior as an attempt to drive her from the pack. Wild canines are shunned by pack members when they are being exiled from the pack. This is a serious, high-stress situation for canines. Shunned individuals release frustration by chewing, digging, barking, or howling. Domestic dogs who feel socially isolated do the same thing, along with urinating and defecating. Because of all these factors, the technique of intentionally ignoring your dog may be one of the stupidest ideas I've heard in a long time!

Obviously, the trainer you worked with knows very little about canine behavior. The unfortunate result is a training method and philosophy that are not taught through a canine point of view, which is essential for teaching canines. Although there may be "many ways to skin a cat," there is only one valid dog training philosophy—and that is to learn to think like a dog and to interact with the dog accordingly.

In addition, the trainer's handling of your golden puppy, Amber, was atrocious. Dragging the frightened puppy to her was essentially an indication of the ego trip she is on. She apparently feels that it is her role to dominate every dog she meets. That's pathetic. An experienced and qualified obedience instructor has the ability to "read the dog" and would not attempt to handle an animal who is frightened and not under emotional control. Instead, the instructor should give clear, precise instructions to the owner and let the owner handle the dog.

Also, good trainers have a way of developing trust in dogs. With time, these trainers usually make friends with even the most insecure individuals. They never force themselves on a frightened dog or do anything to increase the dog's fears.

I'd like to encourage you not to give up on training Amber. Good obedience training will enhance your life and Amber's in many, many ways. But good trainers can be hard to find, despite such efforts as getting recommendations from a vet or a pet boutique (as you did). Keep asking around, particularly when you meet someone with a really well-behaved dog. And if finding a flesh-and-blood trainer fails, pick up a copy of my book, *Dog Talk*. The training program is effective and fun, and it's guaranteed not to traumatize your dog!

Is It Okay to Train with Food?

DEAR DOG TALK: Can you help settle a debate? My friend took a dog obedience course a few years ago with her cocker spaniel. The teacher wouldn't let the students use biscuits or any kind of food during training. We'd like your opinion: Is it wrong to use food when training a dog?

DEAR FOOD-FOR-THOUGHT: No, it's not, and an experienced trainer would not take this view. Food, social interaction between pack members, hunting, and sex are primary canine motivators. I've heard some trainers make the ridiculous argument that dogs lose their ability to think in the presence of food. This is an example of trainers who do not train dogs through a canine point of view. Imagine what would happen to the wolf or coyote if it "lost its ability to think" every time it saw prey! These wily and efficient hunters would all starve to death.

Some trainers take the idealistic view that our dogs should respond to commands solely to please us and that praise should be sufficient reward. The problem with this concept is that it's a myth that all dogs are on earth to please humans. Some dogs *are* very willing to please, and social interaction and praise are enough motivation. Other dogs need more motivation to respond reliably to commands, particularly if, like my dogs, they get free praise just because they are loved.

To use food properly, however, the trainer must be sure that the training program and techniques being used do not make the dog food-dependent. For example, you don't want your dog to respond to a command—such as "Rover, Down"—by looking at you and demanding to see the dog treat before he considers responding! That's being food dependent, and it's a sign that the dog is not very well trained.

In my training programs, I do use food. Its purpose is primarily to be an object of attraction. This means that the food is used to induce, or lure, the dog to do the behavior that I'm helping him learn.

Here's an example: One of the exercises I teach is down-on-command. One of the teaching steps during training involves showing the dog an object of attraction (which actually can be anything the dog likes, such as a biscuit, tennis ball, squeaky toy, etc.—but not the cat!). I show him the object and say "Down" as I lower the object toward the floor. Most dogs follow the object and lie down (provided you place one hand on his shoulder to keep his backside on the floor, preventing him from standing up).

How do I avoid making the dog dependent on food? After I've moved beyond the teaching steps, I reach the testing phase of training. During this phase, the dog learns to respond to a command to earn praise but also to avoid a correction. The corrections are never harsh or abusive. They are what behaviorists call "negative motivators," which the dog wants to avoid.

Sometimes I do reward my dog with food during the testing phase. When I do, the food rewards are staggered, meaning he doesn't get it every time. Also, the dog does not see the food until *after* he has responded.

There is one exercise in which I use food as both a lure and a constant reward. That's come-on-command. I try to make the experience of coming to me as agreeable to the dog as possible. That's because I want the dog to come every time I call him—no matter what the distraction. Food treats are a tool that help to build a strong habit of coming reliably when called.

Trainers who compete in obedience trials often frown on food as a training tool. Why? Because if you call your dog to you in an obedience trial and he comes running, sits in front of you, and then sniffs your hand looking for his food reward, the judge will take off a couple of points. However, that doesn't matter in real life, which many trainers don't seem to understand. If your dog sniffs your hand on the beach, there are no judges taking off points. Actually, you *earn* points in my book! Any dog that comes reliably when called is a true winner.

Polo, a Golden retriever, belongs to a professional fishing guide. Can you tell? One day he put his retrieving instincts to work and helped bring in some of the fish.

So if you find that your dog is food-motivated, you have an excellent tool to shape good behavior. So cut up a hot dog, get out your *Dog Talk* book, and get to work!

A Collar for Sensitive Necks

DEAR DOG TALK: I have a medium-sized dog that I want to train not to pull while walking on the leash. My problem is that Sammy has a very sensitive throat and coughs with just the slightest jerk on a training collar. The same thing happens with a buckle collar.

My trainer suggested a prong collar because it has a pinching effect and does not tighten or put pressure on the dog's throat. I tried this, but every time I jerked the prong collar, Sammy yipped. I think she's too pain-

Most dogs can be trained on a metal-link training collar like the one Cozner is wearing (although his is too long). Some individuals—and even some breeds—do best on alternate equipment, such as the No-Pull halter.

sensitive for a prong collar. Are we doomed to never being able to go for a walk on the leash? That would make our lives pretty difficult! Do you have any suggestions?

DEAR PAIN IN THE NECK: I agree with you that Sammy appears too pain-sensitive to be trained on a prong collar, or what I refer to as a pinch collar. Pinch collars are great training tools for the pain-*in*sensitive dog. But if the collar causes the dog to yip, it should not be used. Yipping is an indication that the dog is being overcorrected. When your dog is crying out in pain she is not under emotional control, and when a dog in out of emotional control, it is not capable of learning.

What I suggest you try with Sammy is a training tool called a No-Pull halter. Don't confuse the No-Pull halter with a traditional halter. A traditional halter is designed for dogs to pull. They are used with huskies to pull sleds, with bloodhounds to track lost people and criminals, and with guide dogs to lead the blind. A No-Pull halter is designed to train dogs to walk on a leash *without* pulling. Also, don't confuse the No-Pull halter with a device called a Halti. A Halti is a halter that fits around the dog's head and muzzle. It is used to lead him around like a horse and, in my opinion, is completely useless as a training tool.

The No-Pull halter has a collar that looks like a buckle collar. It has plastic rings at the front and back of the collar through which elastic cords travel. The cords run from the front of the collar, under the dog's front legs (his "armpits"), to the back of the collar behind his neck. A connecting ring joins them together, and this is where the leash attaches. When the handler tugs on the leash, the cords give a correction under the dog's front legs. The No-Pull halter avoids putting any pressure on the dog's throat or neck.

I recommend this training device for all dogs that have a sensitive throat. I also recommend it for breeds with pushed-in muzzles, such as the Pekingese and the pug. Because of their shortened muzzles, these breeds usually have breathing difficulties, and I don't want to use a collar that might add to this problem. I also recommend the No-Pull halter to anyone training a dachshund. Dachshunds are notorious for neck and back problems. This halter avoids putting any pressure on their vulnerable spinal column.

Although I prefer traditional training collars for the techniques in my *Dog Talk* training program, I find the No-Pull halter is a useful alternative for the appropriate dog. While a relatively new development, the No-Pull halter can now be found in most pet stores.

Epilogue

On a sunny July day in 1996, I was sitting on a bench in front of the Company of the Cauldron, an outstanding restaurant on Nantucket Island, chatting with its proprietor, Steve McCluskey. Across the street another shop owner spotted me and asked if I minded answering a question about her dog. I never mind "talking dogs" and told her so.

She went on to explain how she had just put a four-foot fence around her yard to keep her dog in. "He jumps the fence! What should I do?" she asked.

My response was, "Make the fence higher."

My friend Steve burst out laughing. "That's the profound advice from the famous dog trainer? How much do you usually charge for words of wisdom like that?"

My advice in that friendly sidewalk conversation was, of course, free. The point of this story is that I could have come up with a lot of behavioral "mumbo jumbo" about dogs and dog training. But that's not my approach. I knew that the shopkeeper really had only two practical options. Her dog *could* learn to avoid jumping the fence if she was able to correct him precisely as the dog was thinking about jumping the fence. However, in that case, the woman would have to stand in her yard whenever the dog was out there and growl *"Nhaa!"* as the dog was *about* to jump. The dog would eventually learn not to jump the fence—when his owner was standing nearby. Chances are good that he would still jump the fence when she was not there—particularly since he had already leaped his way to freedom many times before. So the best solution was quite clear to me: A higher fence would solve all her problems.

Practical, commonsense advice has always been the foundation of my dog-training approach. Over the years, my clients have become real fans of my training, and their comments have been unbelievably complimentary. "This makes so much sense" is probably the statement I hear most often from my students. Each year I hear many times over: "This is the best training course I have ever taken" and "It's so wonderful how you taught me how to be firm without being rough" and "Thinking like a dog works so well, and it's fun!"

Statements like these are what originally inspired me to put my training philosophy and techniques on paper. The results are three comprehensive books that are distinctly different from one another but have the common thread of "training through a canine point of view." And as I demonstrated with the fence-jumping story, they are filled with commonsense advice and dozens of uncomplicated training methods that help owners turn untrained dogs into well-behaved, great companions.

The first book in the series is *Puppy Preschool: Raising Your Puppy Right—Right from the Start!* This book is designed to help prospective dog owners choose an appropriate puppy and to help new puppy owners start their little furballs on the path to greatness.

The second book is *Dog Talk: Training Your Dog Through a Canine Point of View.* This is a training book for owners who are ready to start formal training with dogs four months and older. It covers all the training basics in a step-by-step format that makes training a dog easy, fun, and effective.

The third and final volume of my dog-training trilogy is this book. As you have discovered, it's a collection of questions from people in real-world situations who need some useful advice about their dogs. If I really added up all the interesting, difficult, funny, sad, and challenging questions I've been asked over the years, I could probably fill another two or three volumes!

Many people have told me that my books are the best investment that a dog owner could make for their dog. As a collector of dog training books, I have bought and read (or at least tried to read) every training book that has been published in the past three decades—and many long before that. Using my vast library as a point of reference, I can honestly say that *Puppy Preschool, Dog Talk,* and *Why Does My Dog Drink Out of the Toilet?* are the most comprehensive, easy-to-follow, commonsense dog books ever written. Each of them would be a major asset to any dog owner. Published by St. Martin's Press, they all can be found in most bookstores. If they are not sitting on the bookstore shelf, they can be ordered from the bookstore or directly from the publisher at 1-800-288-2131.

With the publication of these books, my training approach has received national exposure. The response has been terrific. Pet owners from all over the country are saying the same complimentary things that I've heard from my clients over the years. It thrills me that many more dogs are now getting trained in a humane, loving, and effective way. My hope is that thousands of dogs will have better lives because of my books.

I'm not a member of any dog training club or organization—even though I've been a dog trainer for twenty-five years. I also have no affiliation with other dog trainers. My only interest in the dog world (besides loving and enjoying my own dogs) is in helping responsible pet owners train and care for their dogs. I'm also more than willing to help any person who aspires to become a dog obedience instructor.

However, independence from the dog-training community doesn't mean that I haven't been influenced by great trainers. Long before I ever touched my first leash, dog-training pioneers Colonel Konrad Most and Blanche Saunders developed training theories and techniques that are the fundamentals of modern dog training. Their methods have been improved on over the years, but they will never become outdated. As in all professions, fads come and fads go. But trainers who truly know and understand dogs never waver from these fundamentals.

I've also been fortunate enough to witness changes in dog obedience classes. When I first became involved with training in the early 1970s, obedience classes were designed to do little more than heel a dog mindlessly around in circles for an hour. Innovative obedience instructors Joachim "Jack" Volhard and the late Olive Point taught instructors how to develop training programs that offered a structured learning experience for both handlers and dogs. As a result of their influence, time spent in obedience classes can be more productive, and training can be more effective. If you listen closely, you can hear the voices of these four great trainers echoing through the pages of my books.

Although this may be the last book I contribute to the genre of teaching people how to train their dogs, I do see many new writing projects on the horizon. In between fly fishing for striped bass, pheasant hunting with my springer spaniel Crea, sharing dinners with friends, and enjoying life on and off Nantucket Island with my wife and daughter, I still plan to spend time in front of the keyboard indulging in a little "Dog Talk."

About the Authors

John Ross

Trainer, instructor, radio host, and author John Ross has been involved professionally with dogs since 1973. His nationally recognized training approach is uniquely designed to teach owners how to train their own dogs.

John began his "canine career" as an active competitor in American Kennel Club obedience trials. Starting with an Irish setter, he earned fourteen obedience titles in six years—one UD, six CDXs, and seven CDs—on nine different dogs of six different breeds. He worked as a veterinary technician for six years and managed a boarding kennel for one year. John has instructed at the nationally known summer camp for dogs and their owners, Camp Gone to the Dogs, in Putney, Vermont. He currently teaches private and group training classes in Fairfield County, Connecticut, and Nantucket, Massachusetts, conducts workshops and seminars nationwide, and gives lectures and demonstrations to breed clubs, school groups, and other organizations.

John co-authored with Barbara McKinney the well-received, highly readable dog-training books *Dog Talk: Training Your Dog Through a Canine Point of View* (1992) and *Puppy Preschool: Raising Your Puppy Right—Right from the Start!* (1996). Published by St. Martin's Press, both books also appear in Europe in a German translation. John and Barbara also wrote the authoritative "Dogs" section for *The New Book of Knowledge* encyclopedia as well as several articles for *Dog World* and *Nantucket Journal* magazines. John writes a newspaper column, "John Ross' Dog Talk," for *The Nantucket Beacon,* and he has authored several articles and a "Dog Talk" column for *Family Dog Care* and *Fetch!* magazines.

In 1993, John released his training video, "Puppy Preschool," to help puppy owners learn how to handle their new pets. Kal Kan Corporation purchased the video and made it part of their popular "Pedigree" product line. A half-hour television infomercial featuring John (and others) promoting "Pedigree" foods and the "Pedigree Puppy Preschool" video began airing nationally in March 1995.

John also hosts a live, weekly radio program, "Dog Talk," which features training advice, pet-care tips, interviews, and phone calls from listeners. First broadcast in 1988, it expanded in 1991 to Norwalk, Connecticut, on WNLK 1350 AM. The show now broadcasts from the Norwalk station periodically while pursuing national syndication.

In addition, John trains Drifter ("the world's greatest demo dog"), his male Australian shepherd, for various media appearances. Drifter has appeared on the televisions programs *USA Today, PM Magazine,* and *CBS News* and has done photo shoots for *Newsweek* and *Town & Country* magazines. Drifter also appeared in a motion picture, *Memoirs of a Madman,* released in 1993 by Coyote Productions. John's newest canine project is his young dog, Crea, a field-bred English springer spaniel who loves chasing tennis balls and flushing pheasants.

Barbara McKinney

Barbara McKinney has been a professional editor and writer since 1979. She specializes in nonfiction subjects, preparing scholarly material for a general audience. She has an undergraduate degree from Dartmouth College and an M.A. in journalism from the University of Michigan.

Barbara began her involvement with obedience training in 1985 and is an instructor in the John Ross Dog Obedience School. She is the co-author with John Ross of *Dog Talk: Training Your Dog Through a Canine Point of View* and *Puppy Preschool: Raising Your Puppy Right—Right from the Start!* and also co-author with John of numerous magazine articles as well as the authoritative encyclopedia article "Dogs" for *The New Book of Knowledge.* She co-wrote the script for the "Puppy Preschool" video and is the co-host on John's radio show, "Dog Talk."

In 1993 she became the editor of *Family Dog Care* magazine, a nationally distributed publication sponsored by several dog food companies.

Barbara owns two Labrador retrievers. Bentley, a yellow Lab, helps with dog obedience classes. Byron, a black Lab, has appeared in television and print advertisements.

John and Barbara turned their long-time working partnership into a lifetime marriage partnership in 1993. They celebrated the birth of their daughter, Hannah, on July 4, 1995.

Index